The American Collection:
CRAFTSMAN STYLE

165 New Home Plans *in the Arts & Crafts Tradition of*
Fine Craftsmanship, Natural Materials, and Simple Elegance

The American Collection
CRAFTSMAN STYLE

Published by Hanley Wood
One Thomas Circle, NW, Suite 600
Washington, DC 20005

Distribution Center
PBD
Hanley Wood Consumer Group
3280 Summit Ridge Parkway
Duluth, Georgia 30096

Group Publisher, Andrew Schultz
Associate Publisher, Editorial Development, Jennifer Pearce
Managing Editor, Hannah McCann
Editor, Simon Hyoun
Assistant Editor, Kimberly Johnson
Publications Manager, Brian Haefs
Production Manager, Melissa Curry
Director, Plans Marketing, Mark Wilkin
Senior Plan Merchandiser, Nicole Phipps
Plan Merchandiser, Hillary Huff
Graphic Artist, Joong Min
Plan Data Team Leader, Susan Jasmin
Senior Marketing Manager, Holly Miller
Marketing Manager, Bridgit Kearns

National Sales Manager, Bruce Holmes

Most Hanley Wood titles are available at quantity discounts with bulk purchases for educational, business, or sales promotional use. For information, please contact Bruce Holmes at bholmes@hanleywood.com.

BIG DESIGNS, INC.
President, Creative Director, Anthony D'Elia
Vice President, Business Manager, Megan D'Elia
Vice President, Design Director, Chris Bonavita
Editorial Director, John Roach
Assistant Editor, Carrie Atkinson
Senior Art Director, Stephen Reinfurt
Production Director, David Barbella
Photo Editor, Christine DiVuolo
Graphic Designer, Frank Augugliaro
Graphic Designer, Billy Doremus
Graphic Designer, Jacque Young
Production Manager, Rich Fuentes

PHOTO CREDITS
Front Cover: Design HPK1800170 on page 181.
Photo by Dan Tyrpak.
Back Cover, Main and Inset: Design HPK1800166 on page 177.
Photo by David Papazian.

10 9 8 7 6 5 4 3 2 1

Printed in the United States of America

Library of Congress Control Number: 2005938833
ISBN-13: 978-1-931131-54-4
ISBN-10: 1-931131-54-6

8

6

Contents

MODEST, MAGNIFICENT

The facade is a pleasing contrast of intricate details and simple geometry. See more of design HPK1800158 on page 169.

Craftsman homes originated with the 19th-Century English Arts and Crafts movement, but have since incorporated influences from all over the world. In turn, the Craftsman look evolved into several equal categories of design, including a recognizably American style. While some of the homes' characteristics remain universal—front porches, multipaned windows, rectangular columns—others are specific to a particular category.

The Craftsman style's popularity peaked in 1901 with Gustav Stickley's publication, *The Craftsman*. In his magazine, he shared ideas for furniture design and architecture inspired by the Arts and Crafts movement, and sold Craftsman-style home plans complete with interior built-ins, furniture, and color palettes. All of the homes were made with natural, regional materials—shingles, wood, stone—in shapes and textures that played with light and shadows. Other key architectural components included: clean, rectilinear lines; exposed structural and decorative beams; recessed porches and entryways outside, inglenooks and alcoves inside; a central fireplace in the living room; and creative, functional spaces such as built-in benches and cabinets.

Exposed structural elements and stone porch supports typify the Bungalow style. See this larger-than-average variation, design HPK1800133 on page 144.

The word "bungalow" derives from the Indian word *bangla* or *bangala*, which describes the native homes of the Bengal region. The style's high-pitched rooflines and center-hall layout promoted heat to rise and air to circulate, which appealed to the British colonials residing in the region's scorching climate. The British built their own interpretations of the design, but by the time the model reached England, little remained of the original. In the U.S., bungalows were made popular by the architectural team of Charles Sumner Greene and Henry Mather Greene, who gathered much of their influence from Japanese architecture. The two-story (with a third-story pool) Gamble House in Pasadena, California, is considered their "ultimate bungalow" even though it deviates from what many consider the bungalow formula: one or two stories, structural simplicity, understated style, and common/living rooms on the ground level.

Frank Lloyd Wright also used Japanese characteristics in developing his infamous Prairie style. A deep appreciation for nature led him to develop a Craftsman-like, horizontal style that was meant to blend with a prairie landscape. Many of his most well-known homes, such as Fallingwater and the Frederick C. Robie Residence, were large, sprawling designs, but he also designed a line of homes to accommodate Depression-stricken families by omitting attics, basements, and fanciful ornamentation. Most Prairie homes, large and small, include these defining traits: low-pitched rooflines, wide overhanging eaves, a central chimney, combinations of one- and two-story wings, and rows of small windows.

In *The American Collection: Craftsman Style*, we've compiled these designs into three size-specific sections: Homes Under 1,800 Square Feet; Homes 1,800-2,499 Square Feet; and Homes Over 2,500. With these sections, not only can you browse a hand-picked selection of Craftsman plans, but you can easily search through the ones that best suit your lifestyle. So enjoy browsing through an architectural style that has truly become an American classic, and perhaps you can begin building your very own Craftsman home. ∎

Exposed beams and columned porch supports are favorite Craftsman details. Matching the carriage-style garage doors and front entry is a well-considered touch.

PHOTOGRAPHY BY EXPOSURES UNLIMITED, RON AND DONNA KOLB

Natural wood tones, picture windows, and period furnishings complete the elegant great room.

PERIOD PIECE

A carefully detailed exterior traces signature Craftsman themes

tone and siding add color and texture to the exterior of this lovely period home. A covered porch introduces a front entry that leads directly into the living room and continues through to the rear.

The dine-in kitchen and attending nook suggest a contemporary lifestyle.
Note the custom woodwork on the floors and cabinetry.

The open floor plan includes a great room with fireplace, dining area, and large kitchen with island and seating. A wall of windows across the rear of the home offers a view to the outdoors, and conveys natural light to the interior. Sliding doors from the great room lead to a deck that spans the width of the home. Split stairs lead to a second floor, where the master bedroom enjoys angled walls, a large walk-in closet, a garden bath with whirlpool tub, a double bowl vanity, a shower enclosure, and a view of the rear property. In all, simple lines and organic materials are in the spirit of the Arts and Crafts style. ■

plan# HPK1800001

Style: Craftsman
First Floor: 1,160 sq. ft.
Second Floor: 1,531 sq. ft.
Total: 2,691 sq. ft.
Bedrooms: 3
Bathrooms: 2½
Width: 37' - 8"
Depth: 53' - 0"
Foundation: Unfinished Walkout
Basement

ORDER ONLINE @ EPLANS.COM

BASEMENT

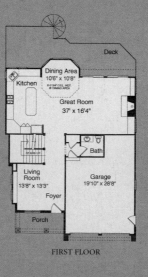

FIRST FLOOR

SECOND FLOOR

Top: The design features elements of the Prairie style, such as cross-gable rooflines and a wide footprint. Above: The island kitchen handles multiple cooks and dine-in guests. Custom cabinetry matches the look of other built-ins found throughout the design.

HOUSE BLEND

A mix of styles produces a unique, beautiful design

Beneath the gently pitched rooflines of this five-bedroom home you'll find a rich blend of Prairie, Craftsman, and Contemporary styles. A full suite of amenities completes the design.

Outside, rustic wood beams—such as the slender porch supports and decorative roof brackets—and stone details establish naturalistic themes. The inside prefers clean, straightforward spaces, such as the combined dine-in kitchen and breakfast nook. On the other hand, the sweeping stairway at the front of the home makes a strong first impression.

Private spaces are more than comfortable. The master suite finds an ideal location at the back of the plan, slightly removed from the rest of the home and provided with views of the rear land-

Above: The front of the plan is designed to impress, highlighting a dramatic stairway and formal dining room.
Left: The master bath delivers modern conveniences, adorned with period details.

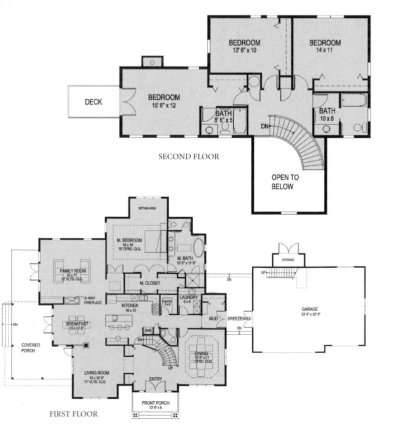

The three-way fireplace between the family room and nook serves both to separate and unify the spaces.

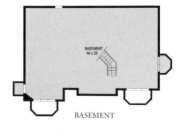

plan# HPK1800002

Style: Prairie
First Floor: 2,554 sq. ft.
Second Floor: 1,742 sq. ft.
Total: 4,296 sq. ft.
Bedrooms: 4
Bathrooms: 3½
Width: 97' - 8"
Depth: 61' - 2"
Foundation: Unfinished Basement

ORDER ONLINE @ EPLANS.COM

scape. Upstairs bedrooms are just as desirable, complete with wrapping views and, in one case, attended by a private deck. ■

BEDROOM
12' 6" x 10

BEDROOM
14 x 11

DECK

BEDROOM
15' 6" x 12

BATH
8' 6" x 5

BATH
10 x 8

DN

SECOND FLOOR

OPEN TO
BELOW

BASEMENT
44 x 29

BASEMENT

SITTING AREA

M. BEDROOM
18 x 19
10' CFRD. CLG.

FAMILY ROOM
20 x 17
12' VLTD. CLG.

M. BATH
12' 6" x 11' 6"

STORAGE

UP

M. CLOSET

3-WAY
FIREPLACE

KITCHEN
16 x 12

LAUNDRY
6 x 6

DN

DN

GARAGE
33' 6" x 25' 6"

BREAKFAST
13 x 12' 8"

MUD

BREEZEWAY

DN

COVERED
PORCH

DN

DINING
13' 6" x 17'
CFRD. CLG.

LIVING ROOM
15 x 15' 6"
11' VLTD. CLG.

ENTRY

UP

FRONT PORCH
13' 6" x 6

FIRST FLOOR

ORDER BLUEPRINTS 24 HOURS, 7 DAYS A WEEK, AT 1-800-521-6797

HOMES UNDER 1,800 SQUARE FEET

For new families and couples just starting out, there are few better homes than Craftsman homes. Designed to be economical and functional, but still stylish and attractive, these small bungalows started appearing in mass among the suburbs of industrial towns and highly populated cities around early to mid-century. They rekindled a desire for economic, single-story living and did so in part by opening the living room up to the dining room through arched pass-throughs or columned, half-wall partitions. The result was a spacious floor plan that encouraged room-to-room flow and accommodated family activities and entertaining.

Because of the designs' modest square footage, these homes include inventive spacing and storage solutions perfect for small families. A partition between the living and dining rooms is the perfect spot for built-in shelves and cabinets, both trademarks of Arts and Crafts style. Use under-stair storage in lieu of basements and attics. Vaulted ceilings and clerestory windows—recently popularized trends—make their mark on single and one-story plans by bringing

in more natural light and creating vertical space. Kitchens evolved, too, with islands, serving bars, and abundant cabinet and counter space. Home owners maintain privacy with either a split-bedroom plan or family bedrooms on an upper half-level, while the master bedroom remains comfortably on the first floor.

You'll be surprised at how much can fit into a plan less than 1,800 square feet. Plan versatility allows bedrooms to become home offices; the dining room can double as breakfast space; you can use bonus rooms for media rooms, game rooms, or an extra bedroom; and don't forget about all of the alfresco dining possibilities on decks and patios. Building a smaller home doesn't necessarily mean settling for less. It just means creatively using space to give yourself more: The Craftsman homes in this section can do just that. ■

Carriage-style garage doors are a good complement to this compact two-story design. See more of plan HPK1800024 on page 33.

This home is distinguished by its two prominent dormers—one facing front and the other on the left side. The dormer to the left boasts a sunburst window that spills light into the family room. Enter through a large covered porch to a foyer that looks into the family room. Beyond, a vaulted kitchen/nook area is graced with an abundance of windows and rear-door access. The master bedroom is located at the front of the plan and is accented with a full bath. On the second floor are two additional bedrooms, each with ample closet space.

plan # HPK1800003

Style: Craftsman
First Floor: 820 sq. ft.
Second Floor: 350 sq. ft.
Total: 1,170 sq. ft.
Bedrooms: 3
Bathrooms: 2
Width: 37' - 0"
Depth: 67' - 0"
Foundation: Slab

ORDER ONLINE @ EPLANS.COM

FIRST FLOOR

SECOND FLOOR

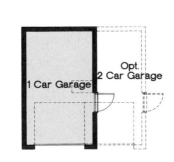

Craftsman detailing lends a rustic feel to this charming three-bedroom home. An ornate covered porch opens to the foyer, distinguished by a decorative column. High ceilings in the dining room and great room are enhanced by abundant natural light. The vaulted breakfast nook is a wonderful place to enjoy casual meals prepared in the angled kitchen. The master suite is situated for privacy with an enticing bath. Two family bedrooms on the opposite side of the plan share a full bath.

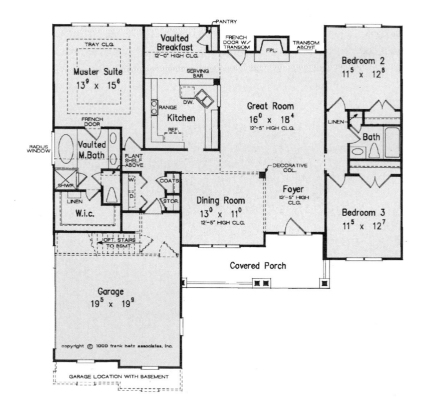

This traditional move-up home will accustom owners to the taste of luxury living. A spacious great room featuring a fireplace and a vaulted ceiling anchors the center of the plan, as well as provides a thoughtful amount of distance between the master suite and kitchen. The suite comprises a spacious bedroom accompanied by a gorgeous bath with dual vanities and compartmented toilet. Built-in plant shelves bring a soft touch to the room. The U-shaped kitchen and nearby pantry are naturally lit and fully functional. Finally, two bedrooms with closets share a full bath.

plan# HPK1800005

Style: Craftsman
Main Level: 1,273 sq. ft.
Lower Level: 47 sq. ft.
Total: 1,320 sq. ft.
Bedrooms: 3
Bathrooms: 2
Width: 48' - 0"
Depth: 35' - 4"
Foundation: Unfinished Walkout Basement

ORDER ONLINE @ EPLANS.COM

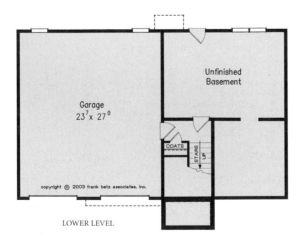

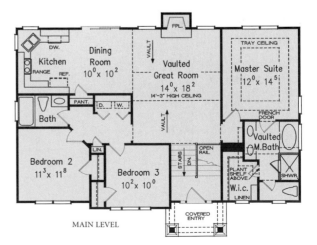

plan# HPK1800006

Style: Craftsman
Square Footage: 1,360
Bonus Space: 397 sq. ft.
Bedrooms: 3
Bathrooms: 2½
Width: 48' - 0"
Depth: 43' - 8"
Foundation: Slab

ORDER ONLINE @ EPLANS.COM

A beautiful arched entrance creates a stunning detail on this traditional wood-siding and brick exterior. Up the stairs from the foyer, the great room impresses with its warming fireplace, handy built-ins, and double-door access to the rear deck. The kitchen is thoughtfully placed between the formal dining room and the bayed nook with a built-in desk. The master suite also opens to the rear deck and features a private bath with an oval tub and walk-in closet. Bedroom 2 also offers a walk-in closet; Bedroom 3 offers built-ins. Downstairs, the two-car garage offers extra storage. A utility room with a bathroom is placed next to a bonus room, which is reserved for future space.

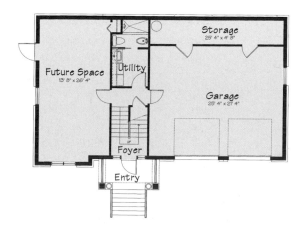

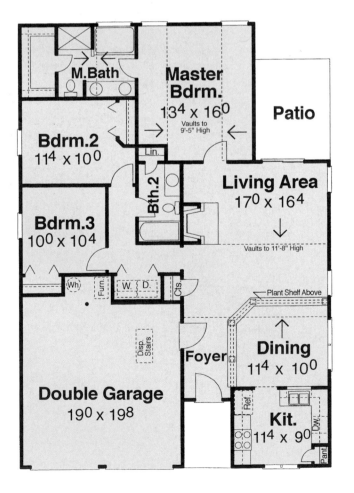

Simple country cottage charm is expressed with carriage-style garage doors on this narrow-lot design. The foyer opens to a living room with a full vaulted ceiling, rising to soaring heights for a feeling of expanded space. The dining area is elegantly defined by columns and a ceiling-height plant shelf. The country-style kitchen features wide windows facing the front property. Bedrooms are designed for privacy; the master suite hosts a dramatic vaulted ceiling and a private spa bath. Not to be missed: a rear patio that is perfect for summer barbecues.

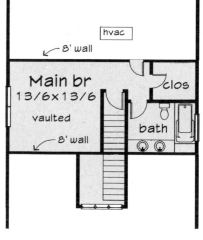

plan # HPK1800008

Style: Bungalow
First Floor: 1,008 sq. ft.
Second Floor: 373 sq. ft.
Total: 1,381 sq. ft.
Bedrooms: 3
Bathrooms: 2
Width: 28' - 0"
Depth: 44' - 0"
Foundation: Crawlspace, Unfinished Basement

ORDER ONLINE @ EPLANS.COM

A quiet, aesthetically pleasant, and comfortable two-story Craftsman home answers the requirements of modest-income families. The entrance to this house is sheltered by an inviting front porch that leads to a spacious living room and allows easy access to the bedrooms on the right. Two family bedrooms on the right share a full bath. The centrally located kitchen is open to the dining room on one side and the living room on the other, which provides an effect of spaciousness. A vaulted master bedroom enjoys a walk-in closet, a full bath featuring double vanity, and all the privacy of the second floor. Designed for casual but comfortable living, this plan showcases a great starter home.

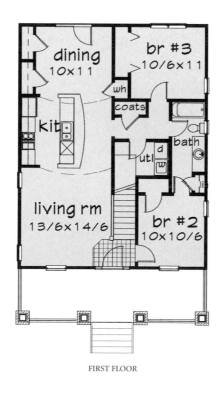

FIRST FLOOR

SECOND FLOOR

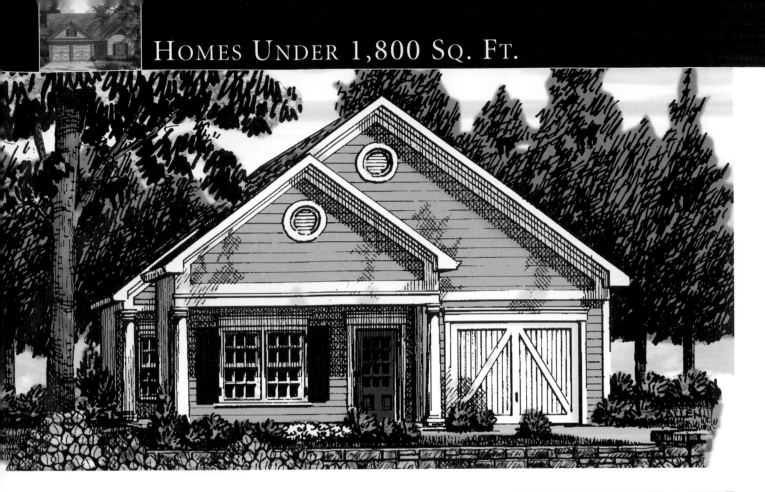

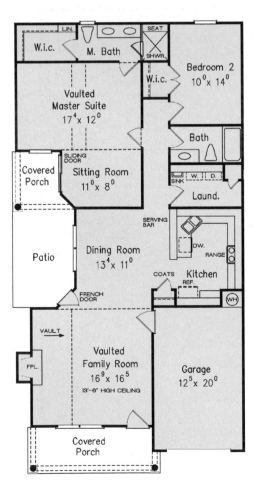

OPTIONAL LAYOUT

Modest living at its best, this unassuming exterior reveals a practical, contemporary design. A fireplace in the vaulted family room warms the space. A side patio and covered porch offers outdoor living space. The kichen bar conveniently serves the adjoining dining room. A hallway leads to the master suite on the left and a second bedroom and hall bath on the right. The vaulted master suite boasts sliding door access to a private sitting room. An optional layout offers a sunroom.

plan# HPK1800010

Style: Bungalow
Square Footage: 1,407
Bedrooms: 2
Bathrooms: 2
Width: 32' - 0"
Depth: 61' - 7"
Foundation: Slab, Unfinished
Walkout Basement

ORDER ONLINE @ EPLANS.COM

Country cottage comfort awaits

the owners of this home. Enter into a spacious, vaulted family room with built-in cabinets, a window seat, and a fireplace with TV niche that is perfect for relaxing. Together with the adjoining dining room this space is great for entertaining and has easy access to a traditional country kitchen with its built-in pantry and separate laundry area. To the rear is a private, vaulted master bedroom suite, a second bedroom, and a second bath. Surrounded by the family room, dining room, and master bedroom, a sheltered patio extends the offer of an outdoor living room.

OPTIONAL LAYOUT

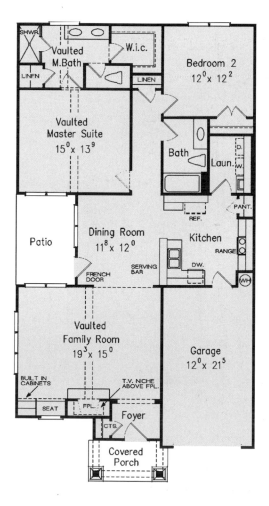

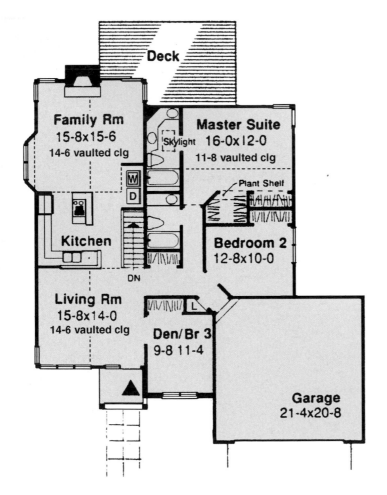

plan# HPK1800011

Style: Craftsman
Square Footage: 1,444
Bedrooms: 3
Bathrooms: 2
Width: 49' - 6"
Depth: 52' - 4"
Foundation: Unfinished Basement

ORDER ONLINE @ EPLANS.COM

Arts and Crafts details jazz up this home's exterior with cedar shingles and open woodwork. An inviting interior starts with the vaulted living room with a row of windows that let in plenty of natural light. The family room opens to the island kitchen. The pleasant fireplace can be enjoyed by those in the kitchen or breakfast area. A short hall leads to the master suite with private bath and a family bedroom. The den can be converted to a bedroom.

© 2002 Donald A. Gardner, Inc.

plan# HPK1800012

Style: Bungalow
Square Footage: 1,457
Bonus Space: 341 sq. ft.
Bedrooms: 3
Bathrooms: 2
Width: 50' - 4"
Depth: 46' - 4"

ORDER ONLINE @ EPLANS.COM

Poised and cozy, this bungalow features a split-bedroom plan, along with half-circle transoms and tall gables on the front exterior. Above the convenient front-entry garage is a versatile bonus room for expansion. Economical and builder-friendly, the floor plan is family efficient and has a variety of custom-styled touches, such as tray ceilings in the dining room and master bedroom. The cathedral kitchen is convenient to the great room, which is highlighted by a cathedral ceiling, fireplace, and French doors that lead to the rear porch. The master suite is complete with a walk-in closet and master bath; an additional bedroom and study/bedroom are located on the opposite side of the house and are separated by a full bath.

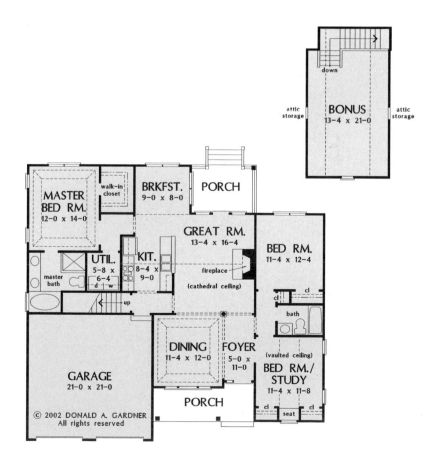

Traditional and Craftsman elements shape the exterior of this lovely family home. The two-story foyer leads down the hall to a great room with a warming fireplace. The U-shaped kitchen includes a window sink and is open to the breakfast nook. A powder room is located near the garage. Upstairs, the master suite provides a private bath and walk-in closet. The two family bedrooms share a full hall bath across from the second-floor laundry room. Linen closets are available in the hall and inside the full hall bath.

plan# HPK1800013

Style: Craftsman
First Floor: 636 sq. ft.
Second Floor: 830 sq. ft.
Total: 1,466 sq. ft.
Bedrooms: 3
Bathrooms: 2½
Width: 28' - 0"
Depth: 43' - 6"
Foundation: Crawlspace

ORDER ONLINE @ EPLANS.COM

FIRST FLOOR

SECOND FLOOR

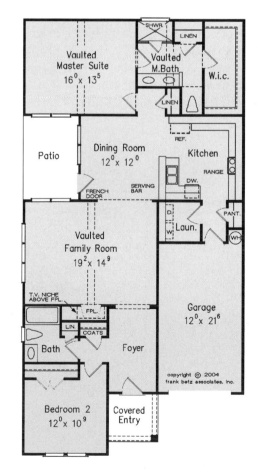

OPTIONAL LAYOUT

plan# HPK1800014

Style: Craftsman
Square Footage: 1,472
Bedrooms: 2
Bathrooms: 2
Width: 32' - 0"
Depth: 63' - 0"
Foundation: Crawlspace, Unfinished
Walkout Basement

ORDER ONLINE @ EPLANS.COM

This narrow-lot plan still manages to feel balanced and coordinated by incorporating great height and flow-through. The vaulted ceilings in the master bedroom and bath and in the family room keep spaces bright and airy. The functional kitchen, dining room, and patio span the width of the plan for ease of use. A full bath attends the second bedroom, located near the foyer for use also as a powder room. The separate laundry room and pantry near the garage are welcome accomodations that shows sensible planning.

© 2002 Donald A. Gardner, Inc.

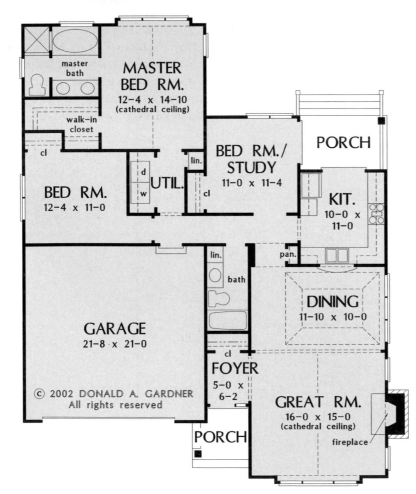

plan# HPK1800015

Style: Bungalow
Square Footage: 1,472
Bedrooms: 3
Bathrooms: 2
Width: 46' - 6"
Depth: 56' - 4"

ORDER ONLINE @ EPLANS.COM

Cedar shake and siding combine with arched transoms to add architectural interest to this Craftsman cottage. A cathedral ceiling and fireplace make a grand impression upon entry to the house as a box-bay window expands the great room. The dining room is distinguished by a tray ceiling. A kitchen pass-through makes serving any occasion easier. Both the kitchen and study/bedroom have French doors leading to the rear porch. The sleeping quarters are located away from the gathering rooms. A cathedral ceiling, walk-in closet, and private bath enhance the master suite.

Ideal for narrow lots, this fine bungalow is full of amenities. The entry is just off a covered front porch and leads to a living room complete with a fireplace. The formal dining room is nearby and works well with the L-shaped kitchen. The breakfast nook opens onto a rear patio. Sleeping quarters consist of a master suite with a walk-in closet and private bath, as well as two family bedrooms sharing a full bath. An unfinished attic awaits future development; a two-car garage easily shelters the family vehicles.

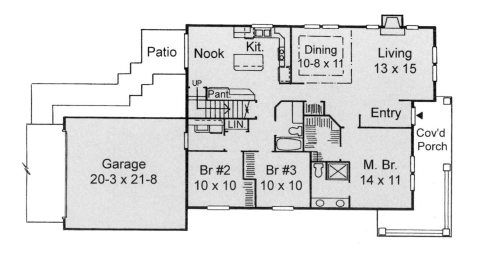

© 1998 Donald A. Gardner, Inc.

B. NATHAN

Rustic on the exterior, this appealing one-story home is a paragon of fine floor planning. Tray ceilings decorate both the dining room and the master bedroom. The great room features a cathedral ceiling and a large fireplace. To pamper the homeowner, the master retreat offers a huge walk-in closet and a bath with a shower, a spa tub, and dual sinks. The breakfast room is set in a bay-window area for sunny, casual meals.

plan # HPK1800017

Style: Bungalow
Square Footage: 1,488
Bonus Space: 375 sq. ft.
Bedrooms: 3
Bathrooms: 2
Width: 51' - 10"
Depth: 58' - 0"

ORDER ONLINE @ EPLANS.COM

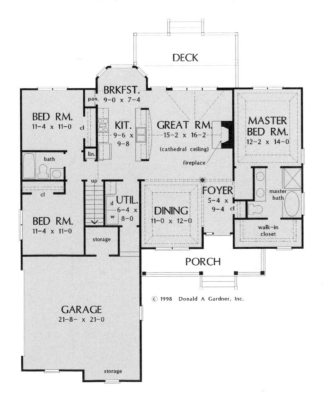

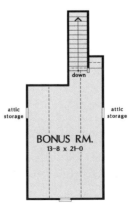

plan# HPK1800018

Style: Bungalow
Square Footage: 1,502
Bedrooms: 2
Bathrooms: 2
Width: 32' - 0"
Depth: 67' - 8"
Foundation: Slab

ORDER ONLINE @ EPLANS.COM

With a classic gabled exterior,

this efficient yet feature-packed design offers a great solution to narrow-lot dilemmas. Vaulted ceilings in the master bedroom and family room bring refreshing height and keep spaces feeling airy. The left exterior insets at the dining room to allow for a courtyard-style patio near the center of the plan. Owners will also appreciate the home's many amenities, such as an oversized walk-in closet, media niches, fireplace, built-in pantry, and compartmented laundry area. Easy access to the garage from the kitchen makes doing chores a breeze.

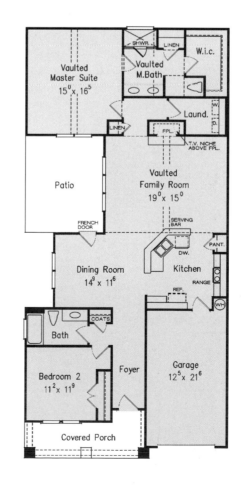

OPTIONAL LAYOUT

Siding and stone with an arched window and cedar siding create a charming exterior on this one-level home. A sloped ceiling in the great room rises two-and-a-half feet above the standard eight-foot ceiling height and a grand opening between the great room and dining area visually expands the living space. A spacious kitchen with an abundance of counter space, a pantry, and snack bar create a delightful place to prepare meals. The master bedroom enjoys a private bath with a double-bowl vanity and large walk-in closet. Two additional bedrooms and a full basement complete this delightful home.

plan# HPK1800019

Style: Bungalow
Square Footage: 1,509
Bedrooms: 3
Bathrooms: 2
Width: 59' - 4"
Depth: 46' - 4"
Foundation: Unfinished Basement

ORDER ONLINE @ EPLANS.COM

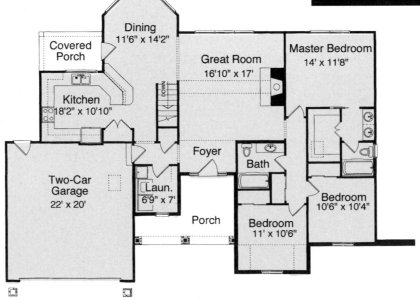

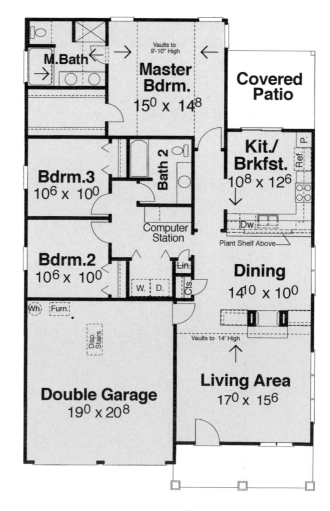

plan# HPK1800020

Style: Bungalow
Square Footage: 1,514
Bedrooms: 3
Bathrooms: 2
Width: 37' - 0"
Depth: 61' - 0"
Foundation: Unfinished Basement, Slab

ORDER ONLINE @ EPLANS.COM

This narrow-lot design creates a cottage style with Craftsman flair; a columned front porch makes a fine first impression. Enter the home to find a living room with a vast vaulted ceiling. A two-sided fireplace defines the space and shares its warmth with the dining room. In the kitchen, a continuous vault and a wide pass-through afford views of the fireplace. To the rear, the covered patio may be built as a sun porch or screened porch. Two secondary bedrooms share a full bath and a computer station. The master suite pampers with vaulted ceilings and a full bath.

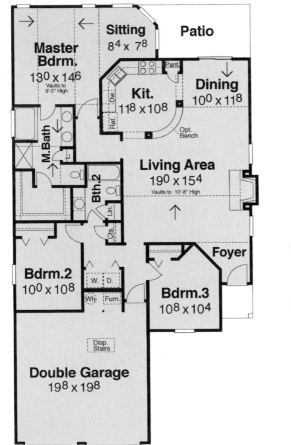

Master Bdrm. 13⁰ x 14⁶
Vaults to 9'-5" High

Sitting 8⁴ x 7⁸

Patio

Kit. 11⁸ x 10⁸

Dining 10⁰ x 11⁸

Pant.

M.Bath

Opt. Bench

Living Area 19⁰ x 15⁴
Vaults to 10'-8" High

Bth.2

Lin.

Cls.

Foyer

Bdrm.2 10⁰ x 10⁸

W. D.

Whr Furn.

Bdrm.3 10⁸ x 10⁴

Opt. Study 10⁸ x 12⁸

Disp. Stairs

Double Garage 19⁸ x 19⁸

plan# HPK1800021

Style: Bungalow
Square Footage: 1,532
Bedrooms: 3
Bathrooms: 2
Width: 38' - 0"
Depth: 66' - 0"
Foundation: Unfinished
Basement, Slab

ORDER ONLINE @ EPLANS.COM

Designed for a narrow lot, this Tudor adaptation provides curb appeal and a great floor plan. The modest front entry is highlighted by a dormer that flows into a cathedral ceiling. Open planning positions the living room, dining area, and bowed kitchen for optimum spaciousness. The curved bar separating the kitchen can accommodate a café-style table, defining the space. The master suite is secluded with a sitting area and splendid private bath. Two additional bedrooms share a full bath near the front of the home.

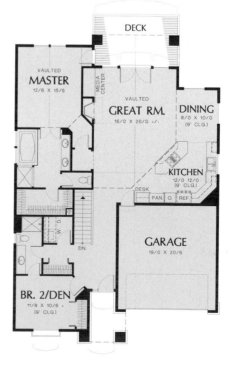

plan # HPK1800022

Style: Bungalow
Square Footage: 1,544
Bedrooms: 4
Bathrooms: 3
Width: 40' - 0"
Depth: 60' - 0"
Foundation: Finished Walkout Basement

ORDER ONLINE @ EPLANS.COM

This Cape Cod design is enhanced with shingles, stone detailing, and muntin windows. The entry is flanked on the left by a bedroom/den, perfect for overnight guests or as a cozy place to relax. The hearth-warmed great room enjoys expansive views of the rear deck area. The dining room is nestled next to the island kitchen, which boasts plenty of counter space. The master bedroom is positioned at the rear of the home for privacy and accesses a private bath. Two family bedrooms and a spacious games room complete the finished basement.

BASEMENT

A covered porch adds instant curb appeal to any style home, and this traditional favorite is no exception. The first-floor master suite is accessible from the entryway. The open layout makes optimum use of the limited space. The kitchen easily serves the adjoining eating area and family room. A rear patio makes alfresco meals an option. Upstairs, two family bedrooms share a full bath. Bonus space on this floor makes a guest room or a game room an option. Extra storage space completes this level.

plan# HPK1800023

Style: Bungalow
First Floor: 1,084 sq. ft.
Second Floor: 461 sq. ft.
Total: 1,545 sq. ft.
Bonus Space: 177 sq. ft.
Bedrooms: 3
Bathrooms: 2½
Width: 38' - 0"
Depth: 61' - 0"
Foundation: Crawlspace

ORDER ONLINE @ EPLANS.COM

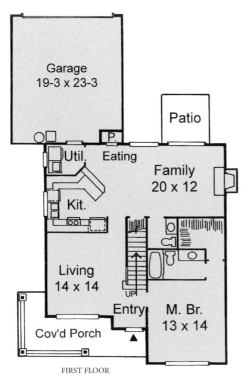

FIRST FLOOR

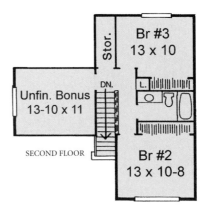

SECOND FLOOR

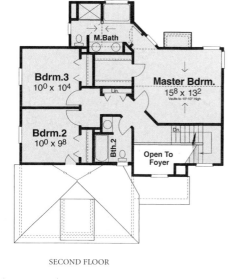

plan# HPK1800024

Style: Craftsman
First Floor: 737 sq. ft.
Second Floor: 840 sq. ft.
Total: 1,577 sq. ft.
Bedrooms: 3
Bathrooms: 2½
Width: 36' - 0"
Depth: 42' - 0"
Foundation: Unfinished
Basement, Slab

ORDER ONLINE @ EPLANS.COM

Loaded with charm, this mountain cottage takes on the ambiance of a country Victorian with rustic appeal. The two-story foyer opens to a sweep-back staircase, lit by a double-hung window. A spacious hearth-warmed living area views the dining room (with rear patio access) and efficient kitchen. To the left, a built-in desk is perfect as a small office or family organization center. Upstairs, a cathedral ceiling in the master suite adds drama; the private bath soothes and relaxes.

FIRST FLOOR

SECOND FLOOR

plan# HPK1800025

Style: Bungalow
Square Footage: 1,580
Bedrooms: 3
Bathrooms: 2½
Width: 50' - 0"
Depth: 48' - 0"
Foundation: Crawlspace

ORDER ONLINE @ EPLANS.COM

This charming one-story plan features a facade that is accented by a stone pediment and a shed-dormer window. Inside, elegant touches grace the efficient floor plan. Vaulted ceilings adorn the great room and master bedroom, and a 10-foot tray ceiling highlights the foyer. One of the front bedrooms makes a perfect den; another accesses a full hall bath with a linen closet. The great room, which opens to the porch, includes a fireplace and a media niche. The dining room offers outdoor access and built-ins for ultimate convenience.

© 1999 Donald A. Gardner, Inc.

plan# HPK1800026

Style: Bungalow
Square Footage: 1,590
Bonus Space: 425 sq. ft.
Bedrooms: 3
Bathrooms: 2
Width: 55' - 0"
Depth: 59' - 10"

ORDER ONLINE @ EPLANS.COM

A cozy front porch and gables create warmth and style for this economical home with an open floor plan and a sizable bonus room. The openness of the great room, dining room, kitchen, and breakfast room increases spaciousness. Additional volume is created by the cathedral ceiling that tops the great room and breakfast area, while a tray ceiling adds distinction and elegance to the formal dining room. Living space is extended to the outdoors by way of a rear deck. The master suite is separated from family bedrooms for parental privacy and features a luxurious bath with plenty of closet space for him and her. Two family bedrooms share a hall bath on the opposite side of the home.

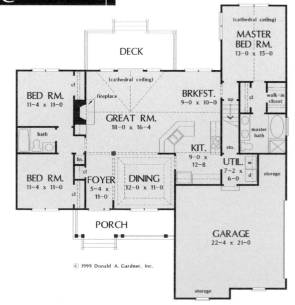

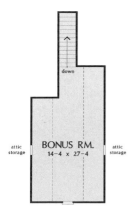

© 1999 Donald A. Gardner, Inc.

This home boasts transitional trends with its charming exterior. The columned entrance introduces the formal dining room and leads to the massive great room with a sloped ceiling and cozy fireplace. On the right, you will find French doors leading to a library/bedroom featuring built-in bookcases—another set of French doors accesses the rear deck. A family bedroom nearby shares a full bath. The gourmet kitchen enjoys an angled sink counter and a breakfast area with a bay window and built-in bench. The secluded master bedroom includes a walk-in closet, a full bath with dual vanities, and private access to the laundry room. This plan includes an optional layout for a third bedroom.

plan# HPK1800027

Style: Bungalow
Square Footage: 1,594
Bedrooms: 2
Bathrooms: 2
Width: 52' - 8"
Depth: 55' - 5"
Foundation: Unfinished Basement

ORDER ONLINE @ EPLANS.COM

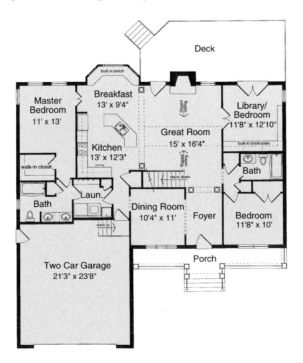

Optional 3rd Bedroom

© 2000 Donald A. Gardner, Inc.

plan# HPK1800028

Style: Bungalow
Square Footage: 1,608
Bonus Space: 437 sq. ft.
Bedrooms: 3
Bathrooms: 2
Width: 40' - 8"
Depth: 62' - 8"

ORDER ONLINE @ EPLANS.COM

This rustic beauty provides a practical floor plan. The great room is warmed by a fireplace and enhanced by a cathedral ceiling. Another cathedral ceiling adds a spacious feel to the master bedroom. Additional luxuries in the master suite include a private bath, two walk-in closets, and access to a covered porch (also accessible from the great room). Two additional bedrooms share a hall bath, with the utility room conveniently nearby. A bonus room is available for extra storage.

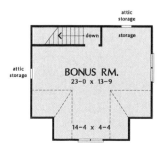

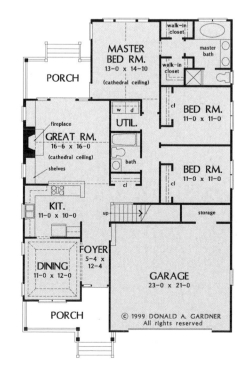

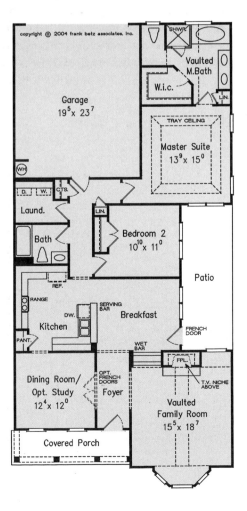

plan# HPK1800029

Style: Bungalow
Square Footage: 1,610
Bedrooms: 2
Bathrooms: 2
Width: 34' - 0"
Depth: 72' - 0"
Foundation: Crawlspace, Unfinished Walkout Basement

ORDER ONLINE @ EPLANS.COM

Perfect fit for a narrow lot, this home offers delicate details. A sweet front porch accents the country cottage facade and large gable roof. The foyer opens to optional French doors on the left for a grand dining room or study entry. Built-ins flank the fireplace and a stunning bumped-out bay adds character and beauty to the family room. A breakfast area connects to the spacious kitchen and a private side patio—a great spot for a garden. Two bedrooms sit to the rear; the master enjoys a private vaulted bath and walk-in closet.

plan# HPK1800030

Style: Bungalow
Square Footage: 1,615
Bedrooms: 3
Bathrooms: 2
Width: 69' - 0"
Depth: 49' - 0"
Foundation: Unfinished Basement

ORDER ONLINE @ EPLANS.COM

A warm and inviting exterior welcomes you to enjoy the beauty and convenience of this one-story home. The central great room is complemented by an 11-foot ceiling, a wall of windows introducing the covered rear porch, and a delightful bar that opens to the kitchen. The dining room enjoys a view to the great room, visually opening these spaces for your entertaining pleasure. Access from the master bedroom to the rear porch creates a private retreat for the homeowner, and the sloped ceiling creates a luxurious atmosphere. The master bath enjoys a double-bowl vanity, shower, and a large walk-in closet. The location of a secondary bedroom allows it to function as a library, if desired.

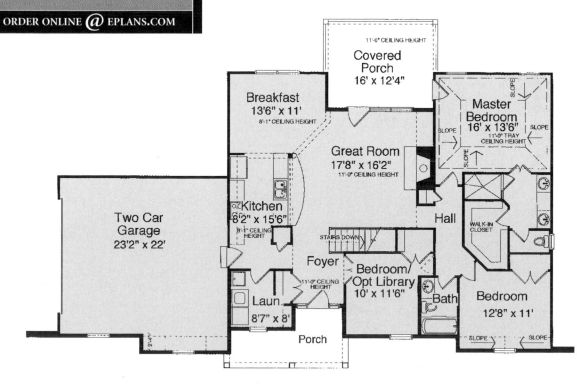

This modern three-level home is just right for a young family. The main level features a study, kitchen, dining room, laundry, and two-story living room with a corner fireplace. A rear patio makes summertime grilling fun. The master bedroom is vaulted and features a double-bowl vanity bath and walk-in closet. Bedroom 2 offers its own full bath as well. The basement level boasts a spacious garage and storage area.

plan # HPK1800031

Style: Craftsman
First Floor: 993 sq. ft.
Second Floor: 642 sq. ft.
Total: 1,635 sq. ft.
Bedrooms: 2
Bathrooms: 2½
Width: 28' - 0"
Depth: 44' - 0"
Foundation: Finished Walkout Basement

ORDER ONLINE @ EPLANS.COM

BASEMENT

FIRST FLOOR

SECOND FLOOR

A distinctive blend of brick and shake shingles introduces this fine country cottage, embellished by multipane windows and flower boxes. The foyer embarks on a plan with raised ceilings and thoughtfully planned spaces. The vaulted great room furnishes a warming fireplace and a French door to the rear property. An angled gourmet kitchen easily serves the breakfast nook and formal dining room, catering to your occasion. Tucked to the rear, the master suite impresses with a tray ceiling, His and Hers closets, and a resplendent vaulted bath with a corner tub. Two secondary bedrooms share a full bath on the far right. Optional bonus space is available upstairs and includes a full bath—perfect as a guest room or home office.

FIRST FLOOR

SECOND FLOOR

With a garage on the ground level, this home takes a much smaller footprint and is perfect for narrow-lot applications. Take a short flight of stairs up to the entry, which opens to a receiving hall and then to the living and dining combination. The living room features a fireplace flanked by bookshelves. The island kitchen and nook are to the rear, near a half-bath. Upstairs are two family bedrooms sharing a full bath and the vaulted master suite, with a private bath and dual walk-in closets.

plan# HPK1800033

Style: Bungalow
First Floor: 897 sq. ft.
Second Floor: 740 sq. ft.
Total: 1,637 sq. ft.
Bedrooms: 3
Bathrooms: 2½
Width: 30' - 0"
Depth: 42' - 6"
Foundation: Unfinished Walkout Basement

ORDER ONLINE @ EPLANS.COM

BASEMENT

FIRST FLOOR

SECOND FLOOR

plan# HPK1800034

Style: Craftsman
Square Footage: 1,641
Bonus Space: 284 sq. ft.
Bedrooms: 3
Bathrooms: 2
Width: 62' - 4"
Depth: 46' - 4"
Foundation: Unfinished Basement

ORDER ONLINE @ EPLANS.COM

A stone and siding exterior, covered porch, and multiple gables decorate the exterior of this popular one-level home. The interior offers a spacious great room with sloped ceiling, grand view to the rear yard, and charming fireplace. The adjoining dining area expands the living space for both a casual or more formal dining experience. A large kitchen with pantry and snack bar organizes the work area. The dramatic master bath with double-bowl vanity, walk-in closet, separate shower enclosure, and large walk-in closet complement the master bedroom suite. A bonus space above the garage creates an area that can be used to best fit your family's needs. Two additional bedrooms and a full basement complete this wonderful home.

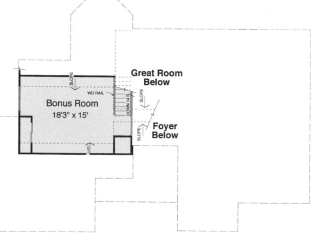

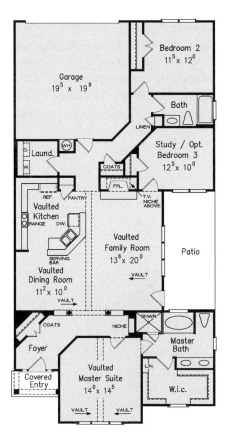

plan# HPK1800035

Style: Bungalow
Square Footage: 1,644
Bedrooms: 3
Bathrooms: 2
Width: 34' - 0"
Depth: 68' - 0"
Foundation: Crawlspace, Unfinished Walkout Basement

ORDER ONLINE @ EPLANS.COM

At just under 1,700 square feet, this traditonal home offers amenities often found in larger homes. Decorative columns distinguish the space between the foyer, dining, and family rooms. Vaulted ceilings outfit the living spaces. The master suite faces the front of the home where it receives abundant natural light. A serving bar in the kitchen is easily accessible by the dining and family rooms. Enhanced by a fireplace and built-in TV niche, the family room offers access to a side patio. A short hallway reveals two additional family bedrooms sharing a full bath, a coat closet, and the laundry room.

Style: Craftsman
Square Footage: 1,651
Bedrooms: 3
Bathrooms: 2
Width: 60' - 9"
Depth: 49' - 0"
Foundation: Unfinished Basement

ORDER ONLINE @ EPLANS.COM

Exterior textured materials and graceful double-entry doors create an inviting atmosphere. A gas fireplace and dual sliding glass doors bring warmth and light to the great room and formal dining area; a sloped ceiling crowns the combined rooms. An open bar separates kitchen work areas from the gathering rooms, yet offers convenience to the living spaces. Split bedrooms offer privacy to the master suite, adorned by a tray ceiling and a lavish bath. Creating a library from one of the secondary bedrooms is a popular option and expands the versatility of the plan. A covered rear porch and full basement provide added benefits to this design.

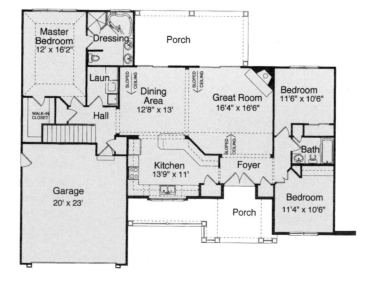

Petite and modern, this Craftsman home fits comfortably in narrow lots and still has plenty of room for the family. Flanking the foyer is the dining room—or make it a study—and a secondary bedroom. The convenient kitchen offers a serving bar and a roomy breakfast area. An open and vaulted family room is cozy with a fireplace and smart with a built-in TV niche. A private side patio is a great spot for outdoor dining. The master suite sits to the rear and enjoys a full bath and walk-in closet.

© 2001 Donald A. Gardner, Inc.

plan # HPK1800038

Style: Bungalow
Square Footage: 1,682
Bonus Space: 320 sq. ft.
Bedrooms: 3
Bathrooms: 2
Width: 40' - 0"
Depth: 78' - 4"

ORDER ONLINE @ EPLANS.COM

This Arts and Crafts cottage
combines stone and stucco to create an Old
World feel. From decorative wood brackets and
columns to arched windows and shutters, the
details produce architectural interest and
absolute charm. This design features plenty of
windows and French doors to invite nature
inside. Built-in cabinetry enhances the interior
and provides convenience. Topping the great
room is a cathedral ceiling, and a tray ceiling
completes the dining room. The master suite,
which features a vaulted ceiling in the bedroom
and an ample master bath, lies next to the
screened porch. A bonus room, accessible from
two additional bedrooms, would make a perfect game room for the family.

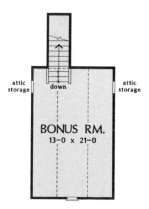

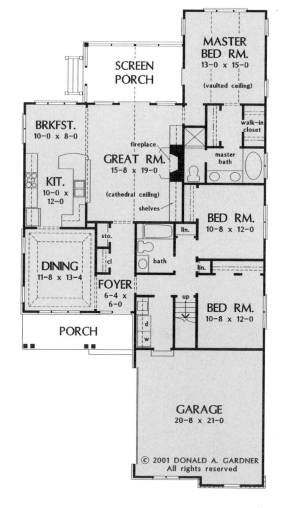

Shingles and woodwork detailing in one of the gables lends a Craftsman aura to this three-bedroom home. Inside, the great room with its fireplace makes a cozy gathering place. The U-shaped kitchen features a serving bar to the dining area. Access the porch via the dining area for informal outdoor meals. A laundry and powder room complete the first floor. Two family bedrooms share a full bath on the second floor near the master bedroom. The master bath features a large soaking tub and walk-in closet. Future expansion is available with a bonus bedroom and bonus study over the garage.

plan # HPK1800039

Style: Craftsman
First Floor: 908 sq. ft.
Second Floor: 799 sq. ft.
Total: 1,707 sq. ft.
Bonus Space: 282 sq. ft.
Bedrooms: 3
Bathrooms: 2½
Width: 53' - 8"
Depth: 33' - 10"
Foundation: Unfinished Basement

ORDER ONLINE @ EPLANS.COM

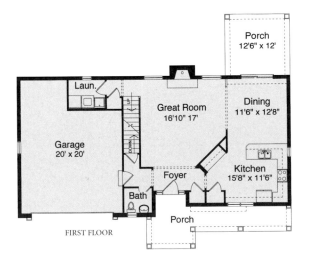

FIRST FLOOR

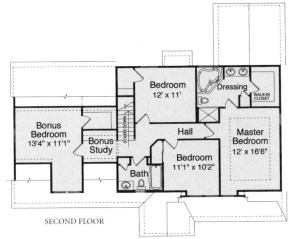

SECOND FLOOR

plan # HPK1800040

Style: Craftsman
Square Footage: 1,724
Bonus Space: 375 sq. ft.
Bedrooms: 3
Bathrooms: 2
Width: 53' - 6"
Depth: 58' - 6"
Foundation: Crawlspace, Unfinished
Walkout Basement, Slab

ORDER ONLINE @ EPLANS.COM

This down-home, one-story plan has all the comforts and necessities for solid family living. The vaulted family room, along with the adjoining country-style kitchen and breakfast nook, is at the center of the plan. The extended hearth fireplace flanked by radius windows will make this a cozy focus for family get-togethers and entertaining visitors. A formal dining room is marked off by decorative columns. The resplendent master suite assumes the entire right wing, where it is separated from two bedrooms located on the other side of the home. Built-in plant shelves in the master bath create a garden-like environment. Additional space is available for building another bedroom or study.

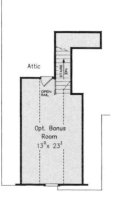

A stone-and-siding exterior brings dimension and color to the exterior of this charming home. A two-story foyer greets you upon arrival, and the great room, with views to the rear and side yards, offers a 12-foot ceiling. The breakfast bay and entry to a covered porch create a bright and cheery place to start the day. Counter space that wraps around from the kitchen provides additional storage and a convenient writing desk. A furniture alcove adds space to the formal dining room and a rear entry hall offers storage closets and a large laundry room. A second-floor master bedroom, with a ceiling that slopes to nine feet, keeps the parents close at hand to younger family members. This home has a full basement that can be developed for additional square footage.

plan# HPK1800041

Style: Bungalow
First Floor: 941 sq. ft.
Second Floor: 786 sq. ft.
Total: 1,727 sq. ft.
Bedrooms: 3
Bathrooms: 2½
Width: 57' - 10"
Depth: 42' - 4"
Foundation: Unfinished Basement

ORDER ONLINE @ EPLANS.COM

plan# HPK1800042

Style: Craftsman
Square Footage: 1,728
Bedrooms: 2
Bathrooms: 2
Width: 55' - 0"
Depth: 48' - 0"
Foundation: Crawlspace

ORDER ONLINE @ EPLANS.COM

A charming dormer window accents the facade of this cozy Craftsman home. To the left of the foyer, double doors open to a den; choose built-in shelves or a convenient wall closet for this room. The central great room boasts a vaulted ceiling, built-in media center, and fireplace, and is open to the dining room, which features sliding glass doors that open to a side porch. A built-in desk adds convenience to the kitchen. Bedrooms to the left of the plan include a master suite, with a private bath and walk-in closet, and one additional bedroom.

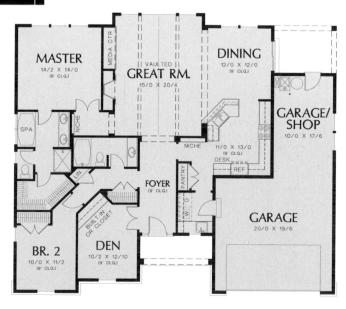

©2001 Donald A. Gardner, Inc.

This combination of stone and siding creates an appealing facade to complement any neighborhood. Inside, the dining room is defined by columns and features a tray ceiling. A fireplace warms up the great room and provides access to the rear deck. In the kitchen, the cooktop island and extended counter space make meal preparation simple and organized. Two family bedrooms—one that can be used as a study—share a full hall bath. The master bedroom provides a private bath with double-bowl sinks, His and Hers closets, a tub, and a separate shower. The utility room is located near the garage entrance.

plan# HPK1800043

Style: Bungalow
Square Footage: 1,753
Bonus Space: 389 sq. ft.
Bedrooms: 3
Bathrooms: 2
Width: 49' - 4"
Depth: 64' - 4"

ORDER ONLINE @ EPLANS.COM

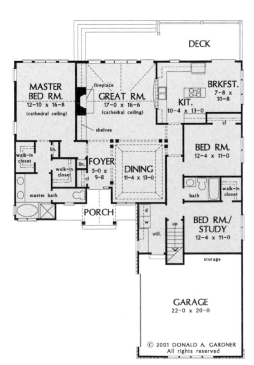

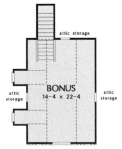

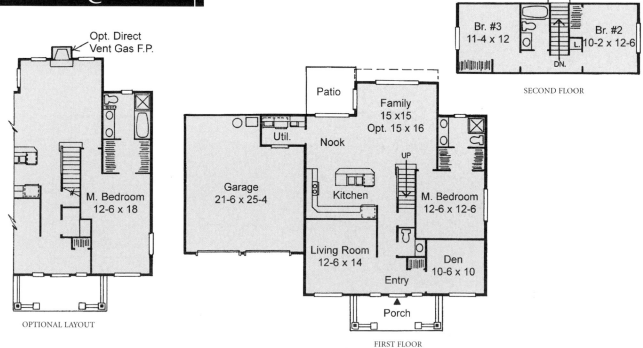

plan# HPK1800044

Style: Bungalow
First Floor: 1,300 sq. ft.
Second Floor: 459 sq. ft.
Total: 1,759 sq. ft.
Bedrooms: 3
Bathrooms: 2½
Width: 56' - 0"
Depth: 46' - 0"
Foundation: Crawlspace, Slab

ORDER ONLINE @ EPLANS.COM

This compact beauty offers ample space and comfort for family living. Three bedrooms—two upstairs and a master suite with a walk-in closet and private bath on the main level—are designed for convenience and charm. An open layout for the kitchen, eating nook, and family room gives lots of flexibility for placement of furniture and other decor. A formal dining room and cozy den are situated in front, just off the foyer. The plan comes with an option for a gas-vent fireplace in the family room.

SECOND FLOOR

Br. #3
11-4 x 12

Br. #2
10-2 x 12-6

DN.

Opt. Direct Vent Gas F.P.

M. Bedroom
12-6 x 18

OPTIONAL LAYOUT

Patio

Family
15 x15
Opt. 15 x 16

Util.

Nook

Garage
21-6 x 25-4

Kitchen

UP

M. Bedroom
12-6 x 12-6

Living Room
12-6 x 14

Den
10-6 x 10

Entry

Porch

FIRST FLOOR

With its brick facade and gables, this home brings great curb appeal to any neighborhood. This one-story home features a great room with a cozy fireplace, a laundry room tucked away from the spacious kitchen, and a breakfast area accessing the screened porch. Completing this design are two family bedrooms and an elegant master bedroom suite featuring an ample walk-in closet. A dressing area in the master bathroom is shared by a dual vanity and a step-up tub.

plan# HPK1800045

Style: Bungalow
Square Footage: 1,759
Bedrooms: 3
Bathrooms: 2
Width: 82' - 10"
Depth: 47' - 5"
Foundation: Unfinished Basement

ORDER ONLINE @ EPLANS.COM

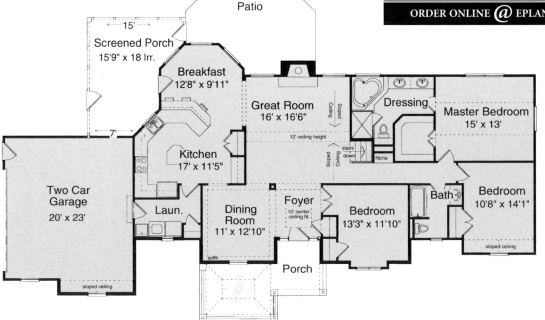

plan# HPK1800046

Style: Bungalow
Square Footage: 1,765
Bedrooms: 3
Bathrooms: 2
Width: 71' - 2"
Depth: 50' - 4"
Foundation: Unfinished Basement

ORDER ONLINE @ EPLANS.COM

Brick, stone, and siding combine with a covered porch to create a delightful exterior on this one-level home. An 11-foot ceiling in the foyer and great room draw your attention to the charming amenities that grace the open living space. A snack bar at the kitchen also serves the great room. The grand opening to the dining room from the great room allows these areas to function as one space. The master suite showcases a high ceiling treatment and enjoys private access to the covered rear porch. The master bath boasts a double-bowl vanity, whirlpool tub, shower, and a large walk-in closet.

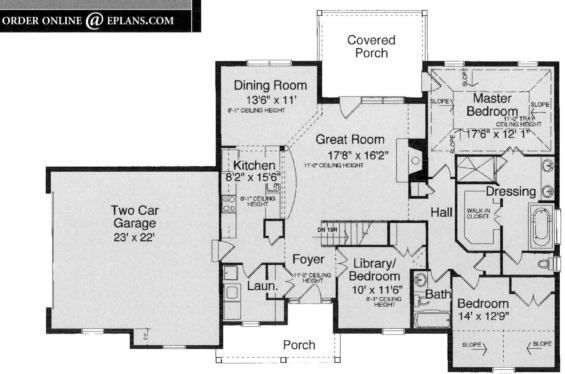

GARAGE
23/0 X 21/6 +

(9' CLG.)
BR. 3
10/6 X 11/4

(9' CLG.)
BR. 2
10/6 X 11/4

VAULTED
DINING
(OPTIONAL DEN)
10/0 X 12/0

D. W.

LINEN

R.

OPTIONAL WALL W/ FRENCH DRS.

(9' CLG.)
NOOK
(OPTIONAL DINING)
10/10 X 12/8

SHLV.

VAULTED
GREAT RM
18/0 X 17/4

MEDIA

VAULTED
MASTER
12/6 X 16/0

plan# HPK1800047

Style: Bungalow
Square Footage: 1,771
Bedrooms: 3
Bathrooms: 2
Width: 50' - 0"
Depth: 70' - 0"
Foundation: Crawlspace

ORDER ONLINE @ EPLANS.COM

Modern amenities and an elegant floor plan define the interior of this design, which offers a classic Craftsman exterior. The vaulted great room, with a fireplace and built-in media center, shares a snack bar with the gourmet kitchen. The nearby breakfast nook includes sliding glass doors. The dining room also boasts a vaulted ceiling; add an optional wall and French doors to convert this room to a cozy den. The master suite, secluded to the right, contains a walk-in closet with built-in shelves, along with a private bath. Two secondary bedrooms to the left of the plan share a full bath and linen closet.

HOMES 1,800-2,499 SQUARE FEET

Craftsman homes may come in select shapes, but they're available in a wide range of sizes. A mid-sized Craftsman home is perfect for growing families or empty-nesters who want to scale down but retain a little extra room for visiting children and grandkids. There are several advantages to living in an 1,800- to 2,499-square-foot home, namely the number of rooms. Not only do these homes usually include a third—or even fourth—bedroom, they also have formal rooms often omitted in smaller designs, which makes them excellent for entertaining family and friends.

The homes in the first section of this book are all about conserving space; the homes here have a little more elbow room. Dining rooms that previously doubled as more casual breakfast rooms have their own place, usually at the front of the home, and can be reserved for special occasions and meals. Formal living rooms can display fine furnishings, artwork, and collections, leaving the hearth-warmed family

or rec room to handle heavier traffic and use. With all of these new rooms occupying the first floor, bedrooms are bumped up to a second level where there's more space for extra bathrooms and more privacy. Greater square footage also pampers the homeowners with larger master suites that spare no amenity: walk-in closets, double-vanity sinks, separate tubs and showers, and compartmented toilets. Even utility spaces feel the effects of more square feet with spacious laundry rooms and the addition of mudrooms and pantries.

Different stages of life demand different home accommodations. Whether you're preparing to move up or ready to take a step back, the homes in this section will provide you with myriad options to suit your situation, whatever it may be. ∎

A signature Craftsman porch creates a neighborly welcome. See more of plan HPK1800090 on page 100.

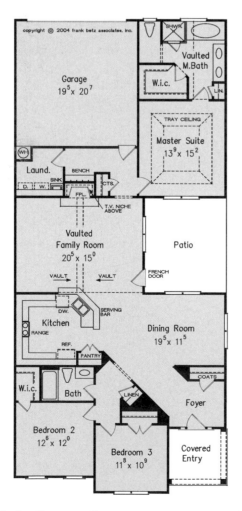

plan# HPK1800048

Style: Bungalow
Square Footage: 1,847
Bedrooms: 3
Bathrooms: 2
Width: 34' - 0"
Depth: 76' - 0"
Foundation: Slab

ORDER ONLINE @ EPLANS.COM

Compact yet contemporary, this Craftsman home fits comfortably in narrow lots while maintaining a modern feel using an open design. The foyer gives way to the spacious dining room with windows lining two walls, one with a view of the rear patio. A serving bar in the adjoining kitchen caters to both rooms. The vaulted family room is enhanced by a fireplace and a built-in TV niche. The master suite, adorned with a tray ceiling, features a dual-sink vanity, a separate shower and tub, and a large walk-in closet. The area outside the master suite serves as a mudroom, complete with a built-in bench and a second coat closet.

plan# HPK1800049

Style: Craftsman
Square Footage: 1,850
Bedrooms: 3
Bathrooms: 2
Width: 44' - 0"
Depth: 68' - 0"
Foundation: Crawlspace

ORDER ONLINE @ EPLANS.COM

With all of the tantalizing elements of a cottage and the comfortable space of a family-sized home, this Arts and Crafts one-story is the best of both worlds. Exterior accents such as stone wainscot, cedar shingles under the gable ends, and mission-style windows enhance this effect. Three bedrooms are aligned along the right of the interior, situated behind the garage, shielding them from street noise. Bedroom 3 and the master bedroom have walk-in closets; a tray ceiling decorates the master salon. Living and dining areas include a large great room, a dining room with sliding glass doors to a rear patio, and a private den with window seat and vaulted ceiling. A warming hearth lights the great room—right next to a built-in media center. The open corner kitchen features a 42-inch snack bar counter and giant walk-in pantry.

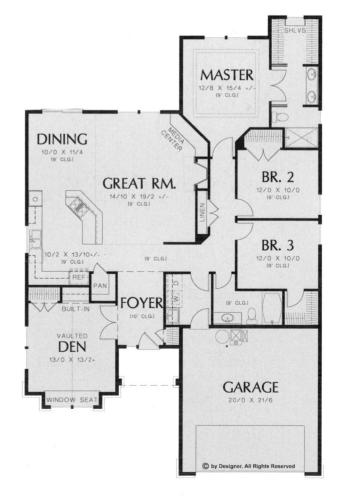

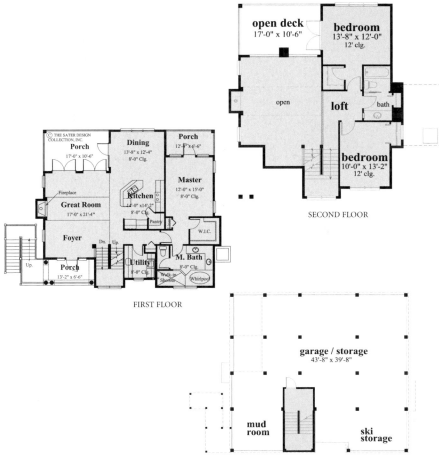

open deck
17'-0" x 10'-6"

bedroom
13'-8" x 12'-0"
12' clg.

open

loft

bath

bedroom
10'-0" x 13'-2"
12' clg.

SECOND FLOOR

© THE SATER DESIGN COLLECTION, INC.

Porch
17'-0" x 10'-6"

Dining
13'-8" x 12'-4"
8'-0" Clg.

Porch
12'-4" x 6'-6"

Fireplace

Kitchen
13'-4" x 14'-2"
8'-0" Clg.

Master
12'-0" x 15'-0"
8'-0" Clg.

Great Room
17'-0" x 21'-4"

Pantry

Foyer

W.I.C.

Dn. Up

Up.

Porch
13'-2" x 6'-6"

Utility
8'-0" Clg.

M. Bath
8'-0" Clg.

Walk-in Shower

Whirlpool

FIRST FLOOR

garage / storage
43'-8" x 39'-8"

mud room

ski storage

BASEMENT

plan# HPK1800050

Style: Bungalow
First Floor: 1,342 sq. ft.
Second Floor: 511 sq. ft.
Total: 1,853 sq. ft.
Bedrooms: 3
Bathrooms: 2
Width: 44' - 0"
Depth: 40' - 0"
Foundation: Unfinished Basement

ORDER ONLINE @ EPLANS.COM

Matchstick details and a careful blend of stone and siding lend a special style and spirit to this stately retreat. Multipane windows take in the scenery and deck out the refined exterior of this cabin-style home, designed for a life of luxury. An open foyer shares its natural light with the great room—a bright reprieve filled with its own outdoor light. Dinner guests may wander from the coziness of the hearth space into the crisp night air through lovely French doors. The master retreat is an entire wing of the main level.

© 2000 Donald A. Gardner, Inc.

plan# HPK1800051

Style: Craftsman
Square Footage: 1,854
Bedrooms: 3
Bathrooms: 2½
Width: 56' - 0"
Depth: 73' - 0"

ORDER ONLINE @ EPLANS.COM

Country Craftsman architecture highlights the facade of this charming family home. A combination of shingles and stone graces the exterior, and interior spaces offer tempting amenities. The foyer leads to the great room, where plentiful fixtures such as the fireplace flanked by built-ins, a cathedral ceiling, and sliding glass doors to the rear porch offer entertainment options. The compact kitchen serves the dining room with ease. The right side of the home provides a comfortable master bedroom complete with a sitting room, two walk-in closets, and a dual-vanity bath. Two additional family bedrooms share a hall bath—one bedroom converts to a study. Finally, a utility room is placed next to the two-car garage with storage.

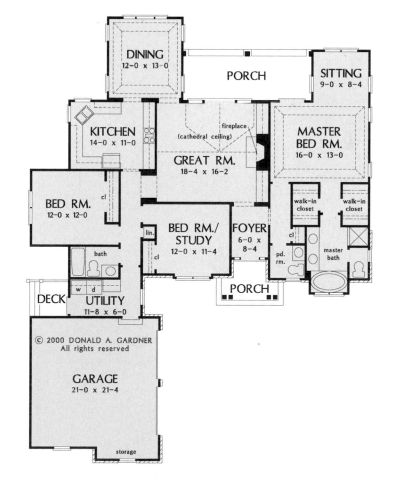

Arched windows and triple gables provide a touch of elegance to this traditional home. An entrance supported by columns welcomes family and guests inside. On the main level, the dining room offers round columns at the entrance. The great room boasts a cathedral ceiling, a fireplace, and an arched window over the doors to the deck. The kitchen features an island cooktop and an adjoining breakfast nook for informal dining. The master suite offers twin walk-in closets and a lavish bath that includes a whirlpool tub and a double-basin vanity.

plan# HPK1800052

Style: Bungalow
First Floor: 1,416 sq. ft.
Second Floor: 445 sq. ft.
Total: 1,861 sq. ft.
Bonus Space: 284 sq. ft.
Bedrooms: 3
Bathrooms: 2½
Width: 58' - 3"
Depth: 68' - 6"

ORDER ONLINE @ EPLANS.COM

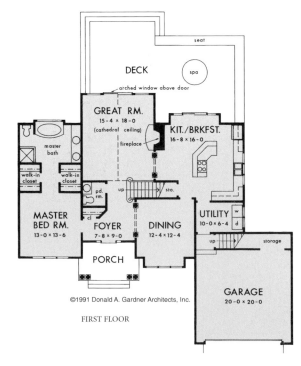

FIRST FLOOR

SECOND FLOOR

REAR EXTERIOR

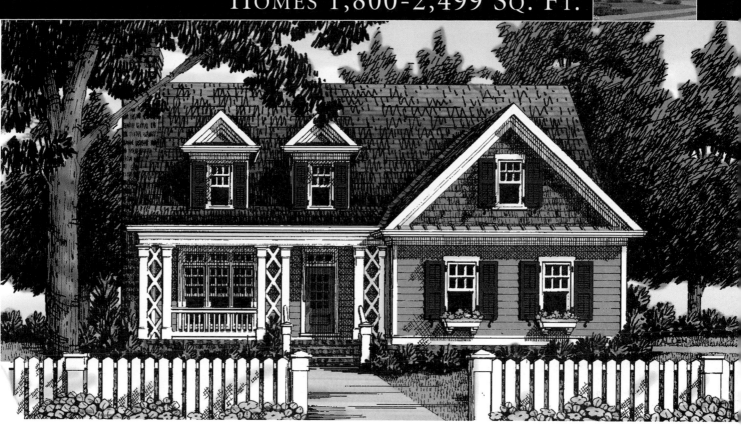

plan # HPK1800053

Style: Bungalow
First Floor: 1,299 sq. ft.
Second Floor: 564 sq. ft.
Total: 1,863 sq. ft.
Bonus Space: 276 sq. ft.
Bedrooms: 3
Bathrooms: 2½
Width: 48' - 4"
Depth: 49' - 0"
Foundation: Crawlspace, Unfinished Walkout Basement

ORDER ONLINE @ EPLANS.COM

Perfect seaside summer cottage or year-round home, this design creates a comfortable space in a small footprint. An open, vaulted family room features a fireplace that can be enjoyed from the adjoining dining room and is a warm center for entertaining. A secluded first-floor master suite enjoys a tray ceiling and a full bath. Two family bedrooms, bonus space, and a full, compartmented bath round out the second floor.

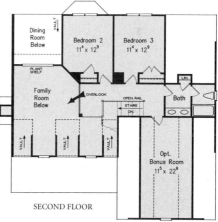

SECOND FLOOR

REAR EXTERIOR

FIRST FLOOR

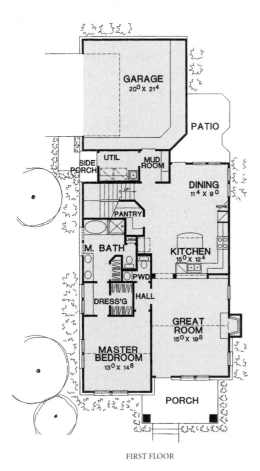

FIRST FLOOR

SECOND FLOOR

plan# HPK1800054

Style: Bungalow
First Floor: 1,297 sq. ft.
Second Floor: 618 sq. ft.
Total: 1,915 sq. ft.
Bedrooms: 3
Bathrooms: 2½
Width: 31' - 10"
Depth: 75' - 10"
Foundation: Crawlspace, Slab, Unfinished Basement

ORDER ONLINE @ EPLANS.COM

This petite bungalow, perfect for a narrow lot, boasts a charming exterior and a practical floor plan. The front door opens directly to the great room, which offers a fireplace. Just to the left, a short hallway leads to the master suite, with its large walk-in closet and private bath; straight ahead are the kitchen and dining room. Special features here include a walk-in pantry, a built-in niche, and access to a covered rear patio. Two second-floor bedrooms, each with private vanity area, share a full bath; a nearby built-in desk provides a convenient space for homework.

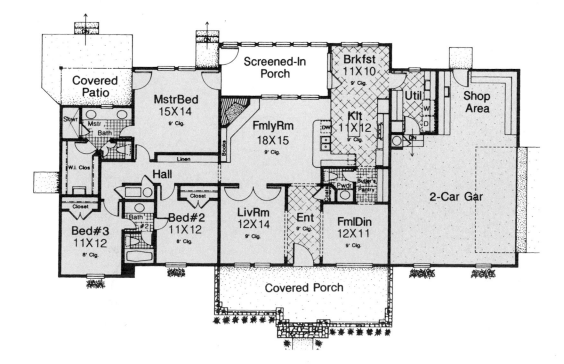

plan# HPK1800055

Style: Bungalow
Square Footage: 1,922
Bedrooms: 3
Bathrooms: 2½
Width: 79' - 3"
Depth: 40' - 0"
Foundation: Slab

ORDER ONLINE @ EPLANS.COM

In the Craftsman tradition, this one-story home is enhanced by rubblework masonry and multipaned windows.

The covered porch leads into the entry, flanked by the living room and formal dining room. The hearth-warmed family room enjoys views to the rear screened porch. The island kitchen provides plenty of counter space and close proximity to the breakfast nook. All bedrooms reside on the left side of the plan. The master bedroom boasts a private covered patio and lavish full bath, and two family bedrooms share a full bath. A unique shop area attached to the two-car garage completes the plan.

SECOND FLOOR

FIRST FLOOR

A Craftsman cottage with careful detailing, this sweet country home is sure to please. From the covered porch, the foyer reveals an open floor plan. The dining room, defined by columns, leads into the vaulted family room. Here, a fireplace framed by windows makes this comfortable space feel cozy. The vaulted breakfast and keeping rooms are bathed in light; easy access to the gourmet kitchen includes a serving-bar island. The master suite features a vaulted spa bath with a radius window and a garden tub. Upstairs, two bedrooms share a full bath.

plan# HPK1800057

Style: Bungalow
Square Footage: 1,939
Bonus Space: 354 sq. ft.
Bedrooms: 3
Bathrooms: 3½
Width: 56' - 0"
Depth: 60' - 0"
Foundation: Crawlspace, Unfinished
Walkout Basement

ORDER ONLINE @ EPLANS.COM

The brick-and-vertical-siding facade lends distinction to this three-bedroom home. The interior is enhanced by columns, transoms, French doors, ceiling treatments and ribbon windows. Amenities galore reign in this home. The elegant master suite boasts a tray ceiling, a French door leading to the private bath which includes a pampering soaking tub and a large walk-in closet. The efficient kitchen includes a breakfast area with a built-in desk, a spacious pantry, and a serving bar. An optional bonus room upstairs adds space.

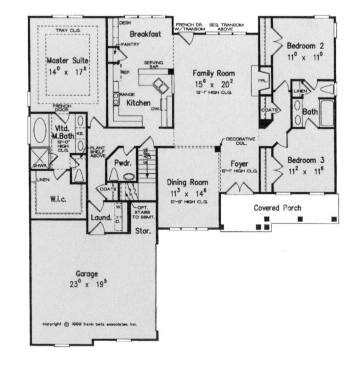

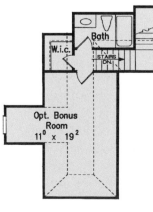

OPTIONAL LAYOUT

Craftsman-style windows decorate the facade of this beautiful bungalow design. Inside, the formal dining room, to the left of the foyer, can double as a study; the family room offers a sloping ceiling and a fireplace option. In the breakfast nook, a window seat and sliding glass doors that open to the covered patio allow homeowners to enjoy the outdoors. The master bedroom dominates the right side of the plan, boasting a walk-in closet and private bath. Upstairs, two secondary bedrooms—both with walk-in closets and one with a private bath—sit to either side of a game room.

plan# HPK1800058

Style: Bungalow
First Floor: 1,305 sq. ft.
Second Floor: 636 sq. ft.
Total: 1,941 sq. ft.
Bedrooms: 3
Bathrooms: 2½
Width: 42' - 4"
Depth: 46' - 10"
Foundation: Slab, Unfinished Basement, Crawlspace

ORDER ONLINE @ EPLANS.COM

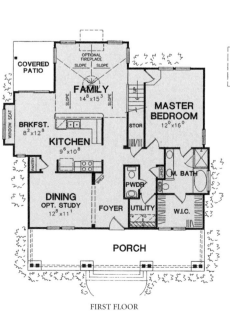

FIRST FLOOR

SECOND FLOOR

plan # HPK1800059

Style: Craftsman
First Floor: 970 sq. ft.
Second Floor: 988 sq. ft.
Total: 1,958 sq. ft.
Bedrooms: 3
Bathrooms: 2½
Width: 40' - 0"
Depth: 43' - 0"
Foundation: Crawlspace

ORDER ONLINE @ EPLANS.COM

A sensible floor plan, with living spaces on the first floor and bedrooms on the second floor, is the essence of this Craftsman home. Elegance reigns in the formal living room, with a vaulted ceiling and columned entry; this room is open to the dining room, which is brightened by natural light from two tall windows. Ideal for informal gatherings, the family room boasts a fireplace flanked by built-in shelves. The efficient kitchen includes a central island and double sink, and the nearby nook features easy access to the outdoors through sliding glass doors. The master suite includes a lavish bath with a corner spa tub and compartmented toilet; two additional bedrooms, one with a walk-in closet, share a full bath.

SECOND FLOOR

FIRST FLOOR

This charming Craftsman design offers a second-story master bedroom with four windows under the gabled dormer. The covered front porch displays column and pier supports. The hearth-warmed gathering room opens to the dining room on the right, where the adjoining kitchen offers enough space for an optional breakfast booth. A home office/guest suite is found in the rear. The second floor holds the lavish master suite and a second bedroom suite with its own private bath.

plan# HPK1800060

Style: Craftsman
First Floor: 1,060 sq. ft.
Second Floor: 914 sq. ft.
Total: 1,974 sq. ft.
Bedrooms: 3
Bathrooms: 3
Width: 32' - 0"
Depth: 35' - 0"
Foundation: Crawlspace

ORDER ONLINE @ EPLANS.COM

FIRST FLOOR

SECOND FLOOR

plan# HPK1800061

Style: Craftsman
Main Level: 1,106 sq. ft.
Upper Level: 872 sq. ft.
Total: 1,978 sq. ft.
Bedrooms: 3
Bathrooms: 2½
Width: 38' - 0"
Depth: 35' - 0"
Foundation: Slab, Unfinished Basement

ORDER ONLINE @ EPLANS.COM

Though this home gives the impression of the Northwest, it will be the winner of any neighborhood. From the foyer, the two-story living room is just a couple of steps up and features a through-fireplace. The U-shaped kitchen has a cooktop work island, an adjacent nook, and easy access to the formal dining room. A spacious family room shares the fireplace with the living room, is enhanced by built-ins, and also offers a quiet deck for stargazing. The upstairs consists of two family bedrooms sharing a full bath and a vaulted master suite complete with a walk-in closet and sumptuous bath. A two-car, drive-under garage has plenty of room for storage.

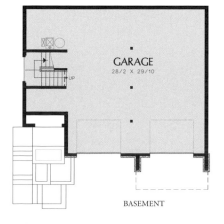

BASEMENT

MAIN LEVEL

UPPER LEVEL

Many fine features mark this one-story country cottage, not least of which are the handsome columns in the front entry and the spacious rear deck. Inside, built-in media centers in the master suite and great room are convenient and attractive. The master suite also boasts a walk-in closet and lavish, amenity-filled bath. The great room, with a corner fireplace, is separated from the kitchen by a curved counter and from the formal dining area by a single column. A handy laundry opens both to the kitchen and the two-car garage.

plan # HPK1800062

Style: Bungalow
Square Footage: 1,979
Bedrooms: 3
Bathrooms: 2
Width: 67' - 2"
Depth: 44' - 2"
Foundation: Unfinished Walkout Basement

ORDER ONLINE @ EPLANS.COM

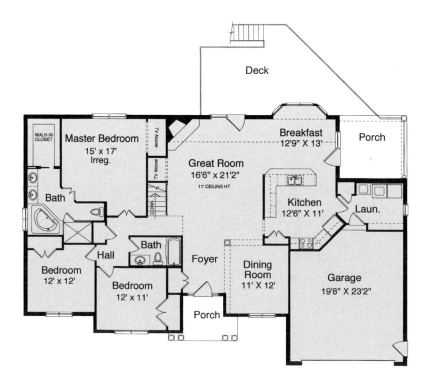

plan# HPK1800063

Style: Bungalow
Square Footage: 1,979
Bedrooms: 3
Bathrooms: 2
Width: 67' - 2"
Depth: 44' - 2"
Foundation: Unfinished Walkout
Basement

ORDER ONLINE @ EPLANS.COM

A brick and stone facade conceals a one-story home lacking none of the amenities of a larger home. A covered porch welcomes guests to the foyer with an 11-foot ceiling that ushers them into the incredible great room. Access to the rear deck and rear porch from the great room and breakfast area, respectively, provide the option for outdoor dining and entertaining. The kitchen is cleverly situated behind the nook via a C-shaped prep island/snack bar. With three bedrooms and spacious room dimensions throughout, there is plenty of room for the entire family and guests.

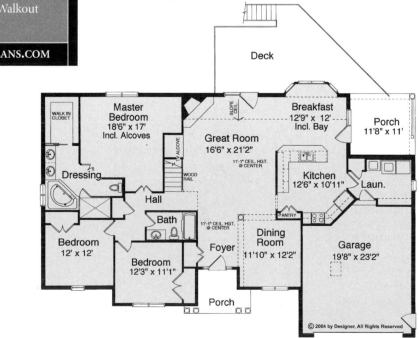

Don't be fooled by the small-looking exterior. This plan offers three bedrooms and plenty of living space. Notice that the screened porch leads to a rear terrace with access to the breakfast room. A living room/dining room combination adds spaciousness to the floor plan. Other welcome amenities include boxed windows in the breakfast room and dining room, a fireplace in the living room, a planning desk and pass-through snack bar in the kitchen, a whirlpool tub in the master bath, and an open two-story foyer. The thoughtfully placed flower box, beyond the kitchen window above the sink, adds a home-spun touch to this already comfortable design.

plan⊕ HPK1800064

L

Style: Craftsman
First Floor: 1,111 sq. ft.
Second Floor: 886 sq. ft.
Total: 1,997 sq. ft.
Bedrooms: 3
Bathrooms: 2½
Width: 32' - 8"
Depth: 50' - 0"
Foundation: Unfinished Basement

ORDER ONLINE @ EPLANS.COM

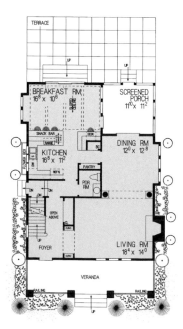

FIRST FLOOR

SECOND FLOOR

QUOTE ONE®

plan # HPK1800065

Style: Bungalow
Square Footage: 2,073
Bonus Space: 350 sq. ft.
Bedrooms: 3
Bathrooms: 2½
Width: 59' - 0"
Depth: 57' - 0"
Foundation: Crawlspace, Unfinished Walkout Basement

ORDER ONLINE @ EPLANS.COM

This handsome bungalow breathes comfort—from the stately columns framing the front covered porch to the family-friendly interior. Step into the foyer fitted with a niche for statuary, and either turn left into the elegant dining room or go straight ahead into the wide open space of the family room. At the far end, a warming fireplace is flanked on both sides by French doors graced with transom windows. An angled serving bar links this room with the kitchen and breakfast alcove. The luxuriant master suite fills the entire left wing. A coffered ceiling rests above the bedchamber; a vaulted ceiling tops the bath. A huge walk-in closet, His and Hers vanities, a shower with a seat, and radius transom windows overlooking a garden tub highlight the comforts found here. On the other side of the house, two family bedrooms enjoy walk-in closets and share a bath.

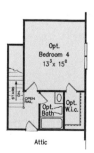

A quaint cottage for seasonal use or year-round, this design is appealing yet practical. The open floor plan combines the living spaces, allowing the kitchen to serve the dining and great rooms and a central fireplace to warm the entire space. The first-floor master bedroom enjoys a dual-sink vanity, a spa tub with separate shower, a compartmented toilet, and a walk-in closet with built-in shelves. Upstairs, two additional bedrooms share a full bath. A workshop area in the garage is an added bonus.

plan# HPK1800066

Style: Bungalow
First Floor: 1,603 sq. ft.
Second Floor: 471 sq. ft.
Total: 2,074 sq. ft.
Bedrooms: 3
Bathrooms: 2½
Width: 50' - 0"
Depth: 56' - 0"
Foundation: Crawlspace

ORDER ONLINE @ EPLANS.COM

FIRST FLOOR

SECOND FLOOR

plan# HPK1800067

Style: Bungalow
First Floor: 1,603 sq. ft.
Second Floor: 471 sq. ft.
Total: 2,074 sq. ft.
Bedrooms: 3
Bathrooms: 2½
Width: 50' - 0"
Depth: 56' - 0"
Foundation: Crawlspace

ORDER ONLINE @ EPLANS.COM

A covered porch opens the way to interior spaces—a main level with living spaces and the master suite and an upper level with two family bedrooms. Designed for the way you live, the great room is vaulted and open to a dining area and handy kitchen. A fireplace warms the gathering area. Corner built-ins in the dining room frame a window and door to the vaulted back porch. The front office also has space for optional built-ins. A side hallway leads back to the master suite. Upper-level bedrooms enjoy the use of a full bath that separates them. A shop area in the garage is an added bonus.

SECOND FLOOR

FIRST FLOOR

A charming country cottage adds curb appeal to any neighborhood. The island kitchen easily serves the adjoining lodge room and the breakfast room offers a bayed view of the backyard and access to a rear porch. The master bathroom is equipped with a dual-sink vanity, garden tub, walk-in closet, private toilet, and shower. Two additional bedrooms each have a full bath. The basement is available for future expansion.

plan# HPK1800068

Style: Bungalow
Square Footage: 2,086
Bedrooms: 3
Bathrooms: 3
Width: 57' - 6"
Depth: 46' - 6"
Foundation: Unfinished Basement

ORDER ONLINE @ EPLANS.COM

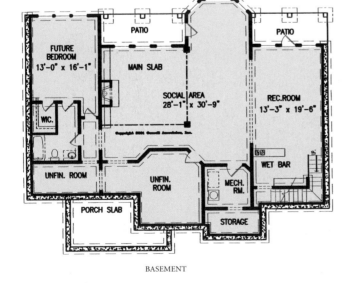

BASEMENT

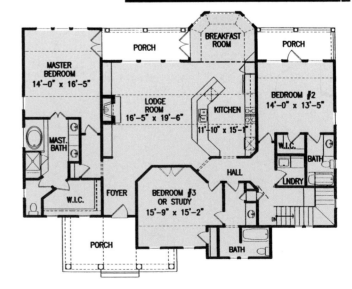

plan# HPK1800069

Style: Bungalow
First Floor: 1,557 sq. ft.
Second Floor: 540 sq. ft.
Total: 2,097 sq. ft.
Bedrooms: 2
Bathrooms: 2
Width: 48' - 0"
Depth: 43' - 8"
Foundation: Unfinished Basement

ORDER ONLINE @ EPLANS.COM

Details make the difference in this darling two-bedroom—or make it a three-bedroom—bungalow. From the front covered porch to the rear porch with decorative railings and stairs, this home offers a sense of comfortable elegance. A gathering room with a through-fireplace offers wide views to the outdoors, and the formal dining room has its own door to the rear porch. To the front of the plan, a family bedroom has its own full bath, while a secluded study—or guest bedroom—offers space for reading or quiet conversation. Upstairs, the master suite offers a through-fireplace shared with a private bath, space for an audio/visual center, and a roomy walk-in closet.

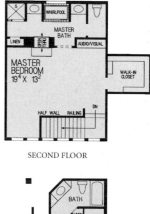

SECOND FLOOR

FIRST FLOOR

OPTIONAL LAYOUT

FIRST FLOOR

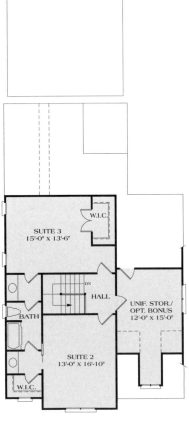

SECOND FLOOR

plan # HPK1800070

Style: Craftsman
First Floor: 1,392 sq. ft.
Second Floor: 708 sq. ft.
Total: 2,100 sq. ft.
Bedrooms: 3
Bathrooms: 2½
Width: 32' - 0"
Depth: 55' - 0"
Foundation: Crawlspace

ORDER ONLINE @ EPLANS.COM

Craftsman stylings grace this two-story traditional home, designed for a narrow lot. Shingles and siding present a warm welcome; the front porch opens to the dining room and the gathering room, allowing great entertainment options. The kitchen connects to the living areas with a snack bar and works hard with an island and lots of counter space. The master suite is on this level and delights in a very private bath. Two bedrooms on the upper level have private vanities and a shared bath. Extra storage or bonus space is available for future development.

plan# HPK1800071

Style: Craftsman
First Floor: 1,032 sq. ft.
Second Floor: 1,075 sq. ft.
Total: 2,107 sq. ft.
Bedrooms: 4
Bathrooms: 2½
Width: 49' - 0"
Depth: 40' - 0"
Foundation: Crawlspace

ORDER ONLINE @ EPLANS.COM

Stone accents combined with stucco and shutters that frame multipane windows add a touch of charm that introduces the marvelous floor plan found inside. The foyer opens to a great room that offers a panoramic view of the veranda and beyond. To the left is a formal dining room; to the right, a quiet den. Just steps away is a sitting room that introduces the grand master suite. The kitchen with a nook, the laundry room, and the large shop area complete the first floor. The second floor contains two family bedrooms, two full baths, and a den/bedroom.

SECOND FLOOR

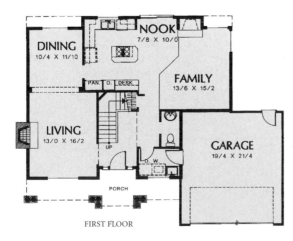

FIRST FLOOR

© 2002 Donald A. Gardner, Inc.

Stone, siding, and jack-arch details create a traditional Craftsman plan you will love to come home to. Thoughtful details, including built-in cabinets, a fireplace, and a snack bar to the kitchen will make the great room a family favorite. Porches off the great room and breakfast nook, one screened and one open, invite outdoor living. The master suite is located at the rear of the plan for quiet and privacy. Here, His and Hers closets and a lavish bath are sure to delight. Two upstairs bedrooms and a bonus room round out this home.

plan # HPK1800072

Style: Craftsman
First Floor: 1,496 sq. ft.
Second Floor: 615 sq. ft.
Total: 2,111 sq. ft.
Bonus Space: 277 sq. ft.
Bedrooms: 3
Bathrooms: 2½
Width: 40' - 4"
Depth: 70' - 0"

ORDER ONLINE @ EPLANS.COM

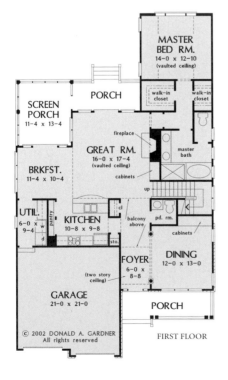

FIRST FLOOR

SECOND FLOOR

plan # HPK1800073

Style: Craftsman
First Floor: 1,561 sq. ft.
Second Floor: 578 sq. ft.
Total: 2,139 sq. ft.
Bonus Space: 238 sq. ft.
Bedrooms: 3
Bathrooms: 2½
Width: 50' - 0"
Depth: 56' - 6"
Foundation: Crawlspace, Unfinished
Walkout Basement, Slab

ORDER ONLINE @ EPLANS.COM

Come home to this delightful bungalow, created with you in mind. From the covered front porch, the foyer opens to the dining room on the left and vaulted family room ahead. An elongated island in the well-planned kitchen makes meal preparation a joy. A sunny breakfast nook is perfect for casual pursuits. Tucked to the rear, the master suite enjoys ultimate privacy and a luxurious break from the world with a vaulted bath and garden tub. Secondary bedrooms share a full bath upstairs; a bonus room is ready to expand as your needs change.

SECOND FLOOR

FIRST FLOOR

Nostalgic and earthy, this Craftsman design has an attractive floor plan and thoughtful amenties. A column-lined covered porch is the perfect welcome to guests. A large vaulted family room, enhanced by a fireplace, opens to the spacious island kitchen and roomy breakfast area. The private master suite is embellished with a vaulted ceiling, walk-in closet, and vaulted super bath with French-door entry. With family in mind, two secondary bedrooms—each with a walk-in closet—share a computer workstation or loft area. A bonus room can be used as bedroom or home office.

plan# HPK1800074

Style: Craftsman
First Floor: 1,561 sq. ft.
Second Floor: 578 sq. ft.
Total: 2,139 sq. ft.
Bonus Space: 284 sq. ft.
Bedrooms: 3
Bathrooms: 2½
Width: 50' - 0"
Depth: 57' - 0"
Foundation: Crawlspace, Finished Walkout Basement

ORDER ONLINE @ EPLANS.COM

FIRST FLOOR

SECOND FLOOR

REAR EXTERIOR

Craftsman details give this traditional home a rustic feel, complete with stone accents and decorative storm shutters. Inside, the gathering room quickly establishes itself as the hub of the home with lots of light and a warming fireplace. The kitchen is created for efficiency as well as beauty, and easily accesses the eating areas with a snack bar overlooking the breakfast nook and a serving buffet just outside of the dining room. Two nearby bedrooms (or make one a study) share a full bath and have convenient access to the mudroom, perfect for keeping dirty boots and sports equipment organized and away from the rest of the home. The master suite is set off to the left for privacy, adorned with a tray ceiling, whirlpool bath, and enormous walk-in closet.

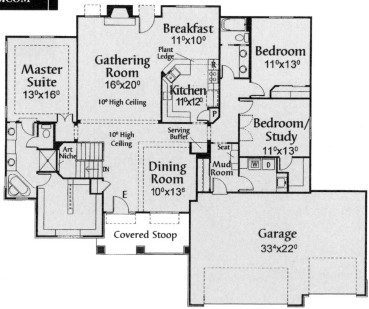

This absolutely appealing Craftsman home dresses up any neighborhood. A deep porch anchored by heavy pilasters is an inviting spot for friends and family. The entry gallery introduces a layout that is open and defines spaces with decorative columns and wall breaks. The dining area looks out onto the front yard and enjoys a view of the fireplace in the gathering room. The island kitchen provides plenty of counter and cabinet space. A sunroom doubles as a breakfast area and has front porch access. Two family bedrooms share a full bath on the second floor. The master suite features a large walk-in closet and resplendent bath. An optional bonus room completes this space.

plan # HPK1800076

Style: Craftsman
First Floor: 1,106 sq. ft.
Second Floor: 1,057 sq. ft.
Total: 2,163 sq. ft.
Bonus Space: 200 sq. ft.
Bedrooms: 3
Bathrooms: 2½
Width: 37' - 6"
Depth: 54' - 0"
Foundation: Slab

ORDER ONLINE @ EPLANS.COM

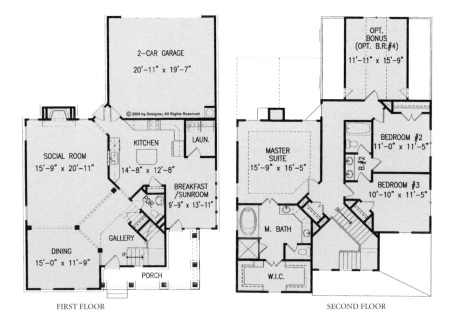

FIRST FLOOR

SECOND FLOOR

plan # HPK1800077

Style: Bungalow
First Floor: 1,455 sq. ft.
Second Floor: 727 sq. ft.
Total: 2,182 sq. ft.
Bonus Space: 727 sq. ft.
Bedrooms: 3
Bathrooms: 2½
Width: 53' - 0"
Depth: 55' - 0"
Foundation: Unfinished Walkout
Basement, Crawlspace, Slab

ORDER ONLINE @ EPLANS.COM

A Cape Cod facade fronts this plan that bridges the indoors with the outdoors. The foyer opens to the dining room immediately to the left, but hides the master suite with an enormous walk-in closet on the other side. A staircase to the upper floor follows, with the vaulted family room at the end. To the left, discover the kitchen/breakfast area, providing proximity to the outdoors via a sunny screened porch. Upstairs confers views upon the activity down below, or opportunities for creative endeavors in the bonus room.

SECOND FLOOR

FIRST FLOOR

Features that make this house a spectacular home include a wraparound porch, stone-and-siding exterior, and a garage that is set to the rear. Splendor continues in the interior, with a large great room that boasts a sloped ceiling, gas fireplace, and a series of windows offering a view to the rear porch. A spacious breakfast area becomes a great place to start the day, with the surround of windows and sloped ceiling. A snack bar and an abundance of counter space create a delightful kitchen. A room set to the front of the kitchen can function as a formal dining room or private study. A bath with shower is convenient to the garage entry. The master bedroom suite is designed to pamper the homeowner in encompassing comfort. Plant ledges and built-in shelves add decorative touches.

plan # HPK1800078

Style: Bungalow
Square Footage: 2,183
Bonus Space: 241 sq. ft.
Bedrooms: 3
Bathrooms: 3
Width: 80' - 0"
Depth: 74' - 0"
Foundation: Unfinished Basement

ORDER ONLINE @ EPLANS.COM

plan # HPK1800079

Style: Bungalow
First Floor: 820 sq. ft.
Second Floor: 1,381 sq. ft.
Total: 2,201 sq. ft.
Bonus Space: 331 sq. ft.
Bedrooms: 3
Bathrooms: 2½
Width: 51' - 0"
Depth: 44' - 0"
Foundation: Unfinished Walkout
Basement

ORDER ONLINE @ EPLANS.COM

FIRST FLOOR

SECOND FLOOR

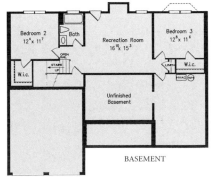

BASEMENT

A stone facade creates eye-catching appeal for this moderately sized cottage. Decorative columns define the dining room, flanked by the foyer. A fireplace in the spacious family room warms the space. Adjacent to the family room, a serving bar in the kitchen provides casual dining in the breakfast area. The master suite, enhanced by a tray-ceiling, features a walk-in closet, roomy bath with dual-sink vanities, separate shower and tub, and a private toilet. The basement houses two additional bedrooms and a recreation room. The optional layout includes a fourth bedroom.

© Donald A. Gardner, Inc.

Cedar shakes, siding, and stone blend with the Craftsman details of a custom design in this stunning home. The plan's open design and nonlinear layout is refreshing and functional. The second-floor loft overlooks a centrally located and vaulted great room, and the breakfast area with a tray ceiling is virtually surrounded by windows to enhance the morning's light. The secluded first-floor master suite features a bay window, tray ceiling, walk-in closet, and private bath. The second-floor family bedrooms are illuminated by rear dormers.

plan# HPK1800080

Style: Craftsman
First Floor: 1,580 sq. ft.
Second Floor: 627 sq. ft.
Total: 2,207 sq. ft.
Bonus Space: 214 sq. ft.
Bedrooms: 4
Bathrooms: 3
Width: 64' - 2"
Depth: 53' - 4"

SEARCH ONLINE @ EPLANS.COM

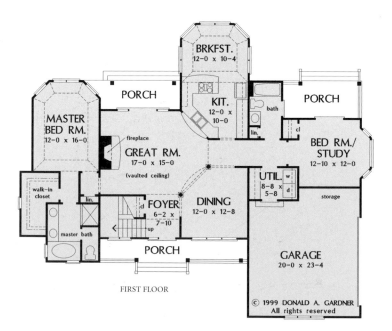

FIRST FLOOR

© 1999 DONALD A. GARDNER
All rights reserved

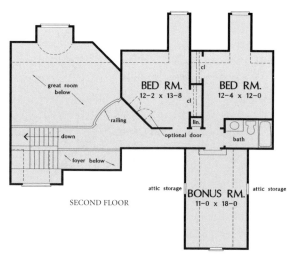

SECOND FLOOR

Cozy and completely functional, this 1½-story bungalow has many amenities not often found in homes its size. To the left of the foyer is a media room, and to the rear is the gathering room with a fireplace. Attached to the gathering room is a formal dining room with rear-terrace access. The kitchen features a curved casual eating area and island workstation. The right side of the first floor is dominated by the master suite, which offers access to the rear terrace and a luxurious bath. Upstairs are two family bedrooms connected by a loft area overlooking the gathering room and foyer.

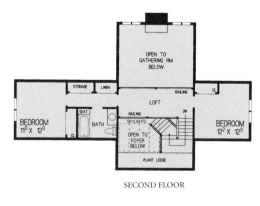

SECOND FLOOR

FIRST FLOOR

© 2001 Donald A. Gardner, Inc.

Stone and horizontal siding give a definite country flavor to this two-story home. The front study makes an ideal guest room with the adjoining powder room. The formal dining room is accented with decorative columns that define its perimeter. The great room boasts a fireplace, built-ins, and a magnificent view of the backyard beyond one of two rear porches. The master suite boasts two walk-in closets and a private bath. Two bedrooms share a full bath on the second floor.

plan# HPK1800082

Style: Craftsman
First Floor: 1,707 sq. ft.
Second Floor: 514 sq. ft.
Total: 2,221 sq. ft.
Bonus Space: 211 sq. ft.
Bedrooms: 4
Bathrooms: 2½
Width: 50' - 0"
Depth: 71' - 8"

ORDER ONLINE @ EPLANS.COM

FIRST FLOOR

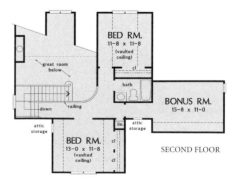

SECOND FLOOR

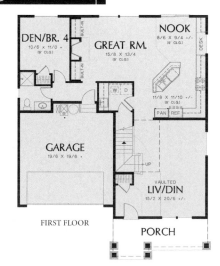

plan # HPK1800083

Style: Craftsman
First Floor: 1,252 sq. ft.
Second Floor: 985 sq. ft.
Total: 2,237 sq. ft.
Bonus Space: 183 sq. ft.
Bedrooms: 4
Bathrooms: 3
Width: 40' - 0"
Depth: 51' - 0"
Foundation: Crawlspace

ORDER ONLINE @ EPLANS.COM

This cozy Craftsman plan conveniently separates living and sleeping quarters, with family living areas on the first floor and bedrooms on the second. The plan begins with a vaulted living/dining room and moves on to a great room that provides a fireplace flanked by built-ins. The adjacent kitchen includes a built-in desk and adjoins a breakfast nook that opens to the rear property. To the rear of the plan, the den can be converted to a fourth bedroom. Upstairs, a master suite—with a spa tub and walk-in closet with built-in shelves—joins two bedrooms and a vaulted bonus room.

SECOND FLOOR

FIRST FLOOR

© 2001 Donald A. Gardner, Inc.

Though the stone-and-siding exterior suggests a rustic nature, the interior offers many refined elements, not the least of which is the lavish master suite. The dining room is accented with a tray ceiling and decorative columns. The great room has a vaulted ceiling, a fireplace, built-ins, and a wall of windows. The island kitchen adjoins the breakfast bay. The front-facing bedroom shares a full bath with the bedroom/study. The master suite includes a bedroom with a tray ceiling, two walk-in closets, and a plush bath.

plan# HPK1800084

Style: Craftsman
Square Footage: 2,252
Bedrooms: 3
Bathrooms: 2
Width: 57' - 8"
Depth: 64' - 4"

ORDER ONLINE @ EPLANS.COM

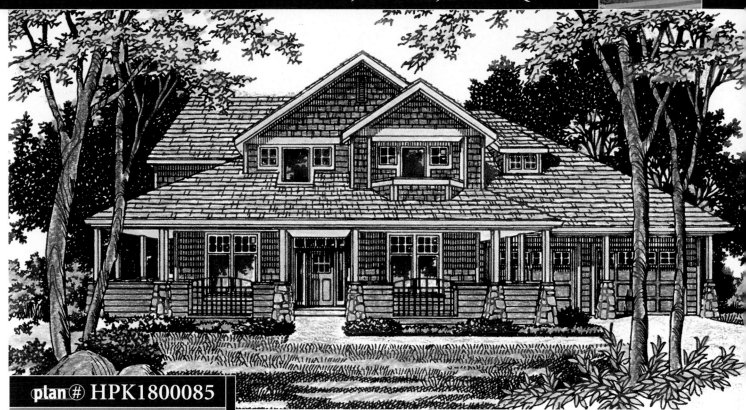

plan# HPK1800085

Style: Craftsman
First Floor: 1,170 sq. ft.
Second Floor: 1,091 sq. ft.
Total: 2,261 sq. ft.
Bonus Space: 240 sq. ft.
Bedrooms: 3
Bathrooms: 2½
Width: 66' - 0"
Depth: 46' - 0"
Foundation: Crawlspace

ORDER ONLINE @ EPLANS.COM

Shingles, stone, and gables are all elements of fine Craftsman styling, beautifully demonstrated on this three-bedroom home. The foyer is flanked by a formal dining room and a cozy den. A galley kitchen is open to the spacious gathering room and sunny, bayed nook. Upstairs, the secondary bedrooms share a hall bath. The master suite is full of amenities, including a sitting area with a private balcony, and a luxurious bath. A bonus room is located above the garage, perfect for a playroom, home office, or guest room.

Balcony

Sitting

M.Br.
18x16

Dn

Bonus Rm.
14x13-6

Dn

Lin

Br.#3
10-8x11

Br.#2
12-6x12

SECOND FLOOR

Gathering
18x17

Nook
9-6x9

Garage
27-8x23-4

Dn

Kitchen

Pantry

Utility

Dining
11x12

Den
12-6x12

Dn

Covered Porch

FIRST FLOOR

This vacation home is certain to be a family favorite. The two-story great room boasts a built-in media center, access to a front deck, and a two-sided fireplace shared by the adjacent den. The spacious island kitchen is ideal for entertaining. The second floor houses the master suite, two additional family bedrooms, and a full bath. A workshop and extra storage space in the garage are added bonuses.

plan⊞ HPK1800086

Style: Craftsman
First Floor: 1,302 sq. ft.
Second Floor: 960 sq. ft.
Total: 2,262 sq. ft.
Bedrooms: 3
Bathrooms: 2½
Width: 40' - 0"
Depth: 40' - 0"
Foundation: Slab

ORDER ONLINE @ EPLANS.COM

BASEMENT

FIRST FLOOR

SECOND FLOOR

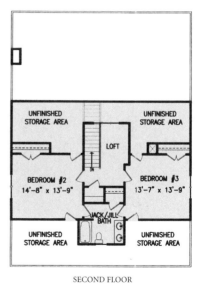

plan# HPK1800087

Style: Craftsman
First Floor: 1,587 sq. ft.
Second Floor: 685 sq. ft.
Total: 2,272 sq. ft.
Bedrooms: 3
Bathrooms: 2½
Width: 38' - 0"
Depth: 55' - 0"
Foundation: Slab

ORDER ONLINE @ EPLANS.COM

With a narrow profile and footprint, this home will fit on the most compact lot without compromising space or amenities. The covered porch is set off by an open, detailed gable, making this a neighborhood-friendly facade. A formal dining room and study flank the foyer and provide ample space for entertaining. The kitchen sports a work-top island and is just a few steps from the spacious family room. The short master suite hall opens to a comfortable and private space with an adjoining sitting room and private bath. The second floor is complete with two bedrooms, loft, full bath, and plenty of storage space.

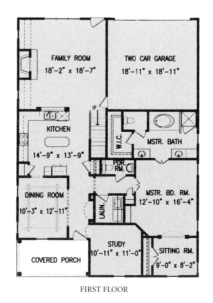

FIRST FLOOR

SECOND FLOOR

The decorative pillars and the wraparound porch are just the beginning of this comfortable home. Inside, an angled, U-shaped stairway leads to the second-floor sleeping zone. On the first floor, French doors lead to a bay-windowed den that shares a see-through fireplace with the two-story family room. The large island kitchen includes a writing desk, a corner sink, a breakfast nook, and access to the laundry room, the powder room, and the two-car garage. Upstairs, the master suite is a real treat with its French-door access, vaulted ceiling, and luxurious bath. Two other bedrooms and a full bath complete the second floor.

plan# HPK1800088

Style: Craftsman
First Floor: 1,371 sq. ft.
Second Floor: 916 sq. ft.
Total: 2,287 sq. ft.
Bedrooms: 3
Bathrooms: 2½
Width: 43' - 0"
Depth: 69' - 0"
Foundation: Crawlspace

ORDER ONLINE @ EPLANS.COM

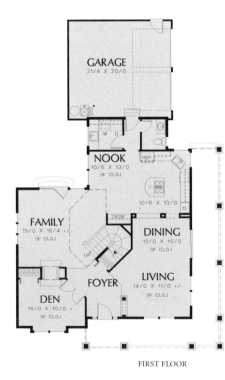

FIRST FLOOR

SECOND FLOOR

plan # HPK1800089

Style: Craftsman
First Floor: 1,675 sq. ft.
Second Floor: 614 sq. ft.
Total: 2,289 sq. ft.
Bedrooms: 3
Bathrooms: 2½
Width: 48' - 0"
Depth: 56' - 0"
Foundation: Crawlspace

ORDER ONLINE @ EPLANS.COM

With a nod to the details of the Arts and Crafts movement, this appealing bungalow has an eye-catching covered front porch, cedar-shingle accents, and light-catching windows. The main foyer separates a cozy den on the left from the formal dining room on the right. A butler's pantry connects the dining room and the convenient kitchen. An angled peninsula containing the cooktop joins the kitchen to a casual nook. There is patio access here for outdoor entertaining. A gas fireplace, skylights, and a built-in media center in the great room create a comfortable place in which to relax. Exquisite in design, the master suite includes a bath with a spa tub, dual lavatories, separate shower, walk-in closet, and compartmented toilet. On the upper level is a hall bath with dual lavatories to serve the two family bedrooms on this floor.

SECOND FLOOR

FIRST FLOOR

Cheerful window shutters and a covered front porch welcome you home at day's end. A two-story foyer sets the tone for indulgence inside, with the formal dining room opening off immediately to the right. A vaulted family room awaits at the other end, affording ambient sunlight through a radius transom. The adjacent kitchen connects to a screened porch through the breakfast area and a French door. A family bedroom is on the other side of the kitchen, with the laundry, a full bath, closets, and garage access nearby. The left wing of the plan is reserved for the palatial master suite, with beamed ceilings in the bedroom, and a vaulted bath. Upstairs comes with two family bedrooms with respective walk-in closets, attic space, and a bonus room.

plan# HPK1800090

Style: Craftsman
First Floor: 1,774 sq. ft.
Second Floor: 525 sq. ft.
Total: 2,299 sq. ft.
Bonus Space: 300 sq. ft.
Bedrooms: 4
Bathrooms: 3
Width: 56' - 0"
Depth: 63' - 4"
Foundation: Crawlspace, Unfinished Walkout Basement, Slab

ORDER ONLINE @ EPLANS.COM

FIRST FLOOR

SECOND FLOOR

ORDER BLUEPRINTS 24 HOURS, 7 DAYS A WEEK, AT 1-800-521-6797

plan # HPK1800091

Style: Craftsman
First Floor: 1,387 sq. ft.
Second Floor: 929 sq. ft.
Total: 2,316 sq. ft.
Bedrooms: 4
Bathrooms: 3
Width: 30' - 0"
Depth: 51' - 8"
Foundation: Crawlspace

ORDER ONLINE @ EPLANS.COM

Perfect for a narrow lot, this shingle-and-stone Nantucket Cape home caters to the casual lifestyle. The side entrance gives direct access to the wonderfully open living areas: gathering room with fireplace and an abundance of windows; island kitchen with angled, pass-through snack bar; and dining area with sliding glass doors to a covered eating area. Note also the large deck that further extends the living potential. Also on this floor is the large master suite with a compartmented bath, private dressing room, and walk-in closet. Upstairs, you'll find the three family bedrooms. Of the two bedrooms that share a bath, one features a private balcony.

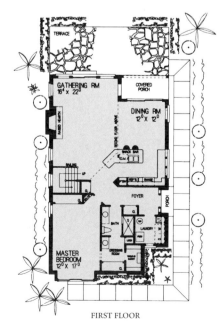

FIRST FLOOR

SECOND FLOOR

REAR EXTERIOR

Fine details like the shed dormer, open millwork accents, an arched entry, and a standing-seam roof will make this home a neighborhood favorite. A split-bedroom floor plan positions the family bedrooms to the left with a compartmented bath between them. The family room, with fireplace and built-ins, is a generous and open space that works with the huge island kitchen, bright sunroom, and breakfast nook. A more formal dining space is found to the right of the foyer. Seclusion is just one amenity the master suite boasts; others include an oversized walk-in closet, super bath, and French doors to the deck.

plan# HPK1800092

Style: Craftsman
Square Footage: 2,326
Bonus Space: 358 sq. ft.
Bedrooms: 3
Bathrooms: 2½
Width: 64' - 0"
Depth: 72' - 4"
Foundation: Finished Basement

ORDER ONLINE @ EPLANS.COM

plan# HPK1800093

Style: Craftsman
First Floor: 1,761 sq. ft.
Second Floor: 577 sq. ft.
Total: 2,338 sq. ft.
Bonus Space: 305 sq. ft.
Bedrooms: 4
Bathrooms: 3
Width: 56' - 0"
Depth: 48' - 0"
Foundation: Crawlspace, Unfinished Walkout Basement

ORDER ONLINE @ EPLANS.COM

Craftsman-style pillars lend a country look to this Cape Cod-style home. An elegant entry opens to the vaulted family room, where a fireplace warms and bright windows illuminate. The kitchen is designed for the true chef, with step-saving orientation and a serving bar to the vaulted breakfast nook. A bedroom nearby is ideal for a home office or live-in help. The master suite is on the left, pampering with a vaulted bath and enormous walk-in closet. Two bedrooms upstairs share a full bath and an optional bonus room.

FIRST FLOOR

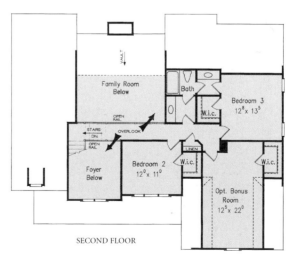

SECOND FLOOR

An attractive combination of styles creates a lovely exterior for this transitional home. The first floor offers a raised foyer and open great room leading to the dining room with a sloped ceiling. Exposed on two sides, a fireplace warms the formal gathering area. A less formal space is created in the island kitchen and breakfast/hearth room combination. The master bedroom is located on the main floor, featuring a sloped ceiling through the private bath with a large walk-in closet, dressing area, dual vanities, and an angled soaking tub.

plan # HPK1800094

Style: Craftsman
First Floor: 1,784 sq. ft.
Second Floor: 566 sq. ft.
Total: 2,350 sq. ft.
Bonus Space: 336 sq. ft.
Bedrooms: 3
Bathrooms: 2½
Width: 59' - 0"
Depth: 67' - 0"
Foundation: Unfinished Basement

ORDER ONLINE @ EPLANS.COM

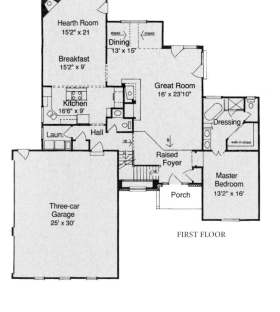

FIRST FLOOR

SECOND FLOOR

This traditional plan, with a hint of Craftsman style, enjoys many charms that will make it a home you'll long to come home to. The country kitchen, for example, is a real delight. It enjoys a handy island counter, a serving bar to the family room, and two pantries—one a butler's pantry, making service to the formal dining room especially efficient. Plant shelves in the upstairs master bath could help make this a semitropical retreat. A downstairs study—or make it a guest bedroom—has hall access to a full bath. Two more second-floor bedrooms with walk-in closets share a bath.

SECOND FLOOR

FIRST FLOOR

This home's multiple-gable facade, front porch, and strong Craftsman accents offer a hearty welcome. The entry leads you right in to the vaulted great room at the heart of the home. A double-sided fireplace warms this room and the hearth room to the left, which connects to both the island kitchen and the casual dining space set in a box bay. A desk and access to the mudroom and laundry room are just some of the kitchen's many conveniences. Taking up the right wing of the first floor is the master suite, which enjoys an enormous private bath. Two additional bedrooms share a full bath and a loft upstairs.

plan# HPK1800096

Style: Craftsman
First Floor: 1,701 sq. ft.
Second Floor: 665 sq. ft.
Total: 2,366 sq. ft.
Bedrooms: 3
Bathrooms: 2½
Width: 52' - 8"
Depth: 56' - 8"
Foundation: Crawlspace, Slab, Unfinished Basement

ORDER ONLINE @ EPLANS.COM

FIRST FLOOR

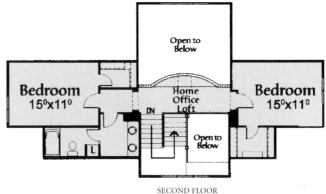

SECOND FLOOR

plan# HPK1800097

Style: Bungalow
First Floor: 1,656 sq. ft.
Second Floor: 717 sq. ft.
Total: 2,373 sq. ft.
Bonus Space: 717 sq. ft.
Bedrooms: 4
Bathrooms: 3
Width: 54' - 0"
Depth: 54' - 0"
Foundation: Crawlspace, Slab,
Unfinished Walkout Basement

ORDER ONLINE @ EPLANS.COM

Twin dormers and a mixture of brick and siding dress the charming exterior of this country cottage. The front porch is bordered by columns and features a trio of arches. Inside, an elongated foyer leads to a vaulted family room featuring a centerpiece fireplace. Tray ceilings crown the master suite, visually expanding the space. The vaulted master bath is complete with a sizeable shower, double vanity, a garden tub, and access to a large walk-in closet. The kitchen offers a serving bar and is conveniently located near the breakfast nook and the laundry room. With the majority of the living space on the first floor, a fourth bedroom, a bonus room, and a full bath on the second floor are great for additional guests or visiting children.

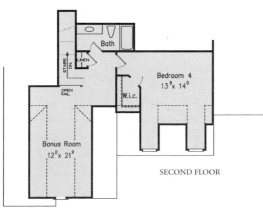

SECOND FLOOR

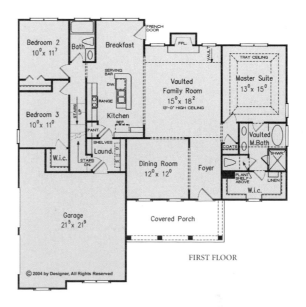

FIRST FLOOR

This three-bedroom home brings the past to life with Tuscan columns, dormers, and fanlight windows. The entrance is flanked by the dining room and study. The great room boasts cathedral ceilings and a fireplace, with an open design that connects to the kitchen area. The spacious kitchen adjoins a breakfast nook and accesses the rear covered veranda. The master bedroom enjoys a sitting area, access to the veranda, and a spacious bathroom. This home is complete with two family bedrooms.

plan# HPK1800098

Style: Craftsman
Square Footage: 2,387
Bonus Space: 377 sq. ft.
Bedrooms: 3
Bathrooms: 2½
Width: 69' - 6"
Depth: 68' - 11"
Foundation: Slab, Crawlspace

ORDER ONLINE @ EPLANS.COM

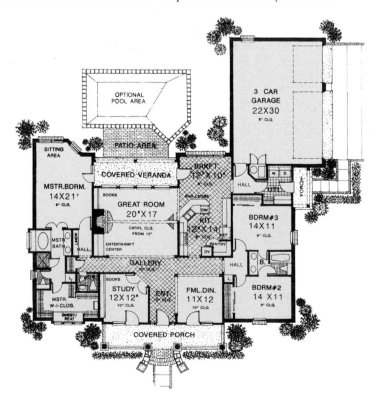

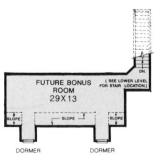

Decorative columns can be found throughout, beginning with the covered front porch. Once inside, the foyer opens to the dining room on the right and the family room straight ahead. Enhanced by a coffered ceiling and built-in cabinets, a fireplace warms the space. A bay window view of the backyard extends private living space to the outdoors. Entry to the vaulted master suite reveals a walk-in closet, roomy bath with dual-sink vanities, separate shower and tub, and a private toilet. A serving bar in the kitchen allows for casual meals and easy interaction between the breakfast area and family room. Two additional family bedrooms share a full bath. Upstairs, a fourth bedroom and full bath, possible guest quarters, and a bonus room complete the plan.

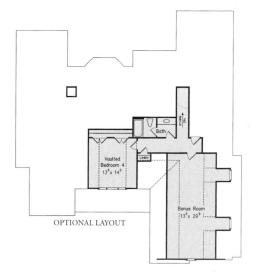

OPTIONAL LAYOUT

A great room with a fireplace, tall double windows, and access to a covered rear porch are highlights of this lovely Prairie-style home. The kitchen—with a walk-in pantry, central island, and plenty of counter space—easily serves the formal dining room. The study, which features a walk-in closet and adjoins a full bath, could serve as a bedroom, if necessary. Upstairs, the master bedroom boasts a full bath with a spa tub and a shower with a built-in seat. Two additional bedrooms share a full bath that includes a linen closet.

plan # HPK1800100

Style: Prairie
First Floor: 1,290 sq. ft.
Second Floor: 1,132 sq. ft.
Total: 2,422 sq. ft.
Bedrooms: 3
Bathrooms: 3
Width: 35' - 11"
Depth: 51' - 5"
Foundation: Crawlspace, Slab

ORDER ONLINE @ EPLANS.COM

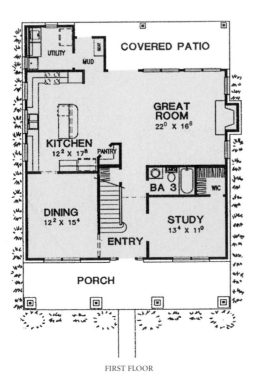

FIRST FLOOR

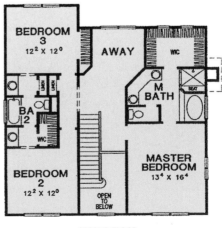

SECOND FLOOR

plan# HPK1800101

Style: Craftsman
First Floor: 1,501 sq. ft.
Second Floor: 921 sq. ft.
Total: 2,422 sq. ft.
Bedrooms: 3
Bathrooms: 2½
Width: 52' - 0"
Depth: 36' - 0"
Foundation: Crawlspace

ORDER ONLINE @ EPLANS.COM

The contemporary look of this modern country design is both impressive and unique. Enormous windows brighten and enliven every interior space. The vaulted family room features a fireplace, and a two-sided fireplace warms the formal living and dining rooms. The gourmet island kitchen is open to a nook. Double doors open to a den that accesses a front deck. Upstairs, the master bedroom features a private bath with linen storage and a walk-in closet. Two family bedrooms share a Jack-and-Jill bath. The two-car garage features a storage area on the lower level.

SECOND FLOOR

FIRST FLOOR

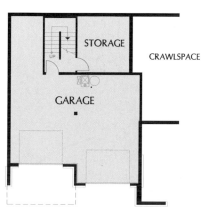

BASEMENT

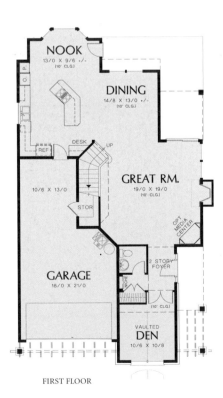

FIRST FLOOR

SECOND FLOOR

ptan# HPK1800102

Style: Craftsman
First Floor: 1,204 sq. ft.
Second Floor: 1,264 sq. ft.
Total: 2,468 sq. ft.
Bonus Space: 213 sq. ft.
Bedrooms: 3
Bathrooms: 2½
Width: 35' - 0"
Depth: 63' - 0"
Foundation: Crawlspace

ORDER ONLINE @ EPLANS.COM

A traditional design with nontraditional amenities, this mid-size home is sure to please. The front-facing den, enhanced by French doors, is bathed in natural light. The great room sits at the heart of the home with an optional media center in the corner and a central fireplace along the right wall. The open design leads nicely into the adjoining dining room and kitchen. An island cooktop/serving bar conveniently serves the area. A future deck is accessible from the breakfast nook. Upstairs, the spacious master suite boasts a dual-sink vanity, a spa tub, a separate shower, a compartmented toilet, and an enormous walk-in closet.

plan # HPK1800103

Style: Craftsman
First Floor: 1,711 sq. ft.
Second Floor: 773 sq. ft.
Total: 2,484 sq. ft.
Bonus Space: 323 sq. ft.
Bedrooms: 4
Bathrooms: 3½
Width: 50' - 8"
Depth: 62' - 0"
Foundation: Crawlspace, Slab,
Unfinished Basement

ORDER ONLINE @ EPLANS.COM

A rustic blend of Craftsman and farmhouse styles envelops a surprisingly comfortable floor plan with an open layout and abundant natural light. A wrapping front porch opens to the foyer that leads to a parlor (or make it a formal dining room). Ahead, the great room is lit by a beautiful arched window and enjoys the warmth of a fireplace. The kitchen and family dining room are assisted by a serving-bar island. A home office is nearby. The master suite is located for privacy and delights in French doors, dual vanities, linen closets, walk-in closets with built-in seats, and a spectacular whirlpool tub and separate shower. Three upstairs bedrooms (one with a full bath and two sharing a bath) access optional bonus space, perfect as a playroom.

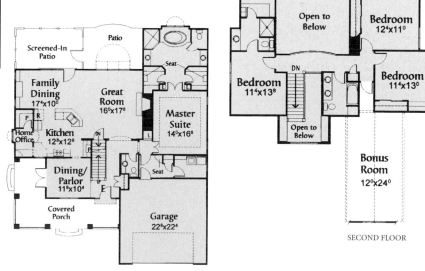

FIRST FLOOR

SECOND FLOOR

This two story home with stone, shake, and siding facade and a side-entry two-car garage presents spectacular curb appeal to this family-sized home. Trim detail and a copper roof enhance the beauty of the exterior. A nine-foot first-floor ceiling height is standard throughout, with the great room and foyer ceilings soaring to a full two-story height. Columns and an arched opening frame the kitchen from the great room and a boxed bay expands the breakfast area. A triple sliding glass door allows an abundance of light in and invites the activities to continue to the rear covered porch. A deluxe master bedroom suite boasts of a whirlpool tub, double-bowl vanity shower, and spacious walk-in closet. From the second-floor balcony, a dramatic view is showcased to the great room and foyer. A secondary bedroom with a private bath makes a wonderful guest room.

plan # HPK1800104

Style: Craftsman
First Floor: 1,710 sq. ft.
Second Floor: 774 sq. ft.
Total: 2,484 sq. ft.
Bedrooms: 4
Bathrooms: 3½
Width: 57' - 8"
Depth: 58' - 0"
Foundation: Unfinished Basement

ORDER ONLINE @ EPLANS.COM

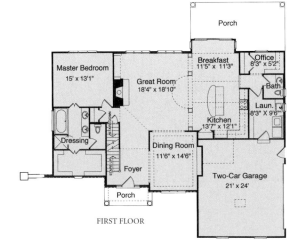

FIRST FLOOR

SECOND FLOOR

Vertical siding and stone details create the facade of this Craftsman home. One story, measuring just under 2,500 square feet, is all you need when the floor plan is as perfect as this one. Family and friends will feel right at home in the family room topped with a gorgeous coffered ceiling and embellished with a warming fireplace flanked by built-in shelves. The nearby kitchen with corner pantry connects to a convenient breakfast room and is only a hop away from the formal dining area. The master suite and bath are spectacular—feel free to turn the living room into a master sitting room for more space. Two more bedrooms are on the opposite side of the plan and share a full bath. The dual sinks here will ensure quick and painless morning/evening routines. A laundry room and powder room provide the finishing touches.

This fine bungalow, with its multiple gables, rafter tails, and pillared front porch, will be the envy of any neighborhood. A beam-ceilinged great room is further enhanced by a through-fireplace and French doors to the rear terrace. The U-shaped kitchen features a cooktop island with a snack bar and offers a beam-ceilinged breakfast/keeping room that shares the through-fireplace with the great room. Two secondary bedrooms share a full bath; the master suite is designed to pamper. Here, the homeowner will be pleased with a walk-in closet, a separate shower, and access to the terrace. The two-car garage has a side entrance and will easily shelter the family fleet.

plan # HPK1800106

Style: Bungalow
Square Footage: 2,489
Bedrooms: 3
Bathrooms: 2½
Width: 68' - 3"
Depth: 62' - 0"
Foundation: Walkout Basement

ORDER ONLINE @ EPLANS.COM

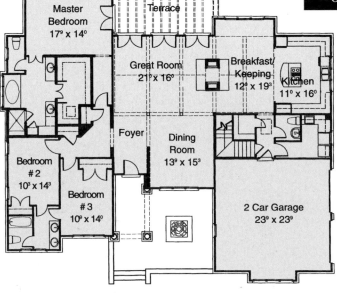

HOMES OVER 2,500 SQUARE FEET

When Craftsman homes became popular among the middle class at the turn of the 20th Century, they also attracted the attention of the wealthy upper class. Growing tired of the turrets and unnecessary ornamentation of Victorian homes, this society saw the designs as an opportunity to return to a simpler style. Natural building materials, such as stone and wood, made Craftsman homes ideal for the class's several-thousand-square-foot, rustic vacation "cottages." Several years later, Frank Lloyd Wright adapted these home styles and developed the celebrated Prairie style. While his designs were more modern than rustic, they still exemplify how Craftsman characteristics from the original, modestly-sized bungalows can be applied to much larger structures.

Certain traits on a home's façade can give it a distinct Craftsman appeal. A front porch, large or small, at the entry is a must-have; the home should definitely have columns, and likely a brick half-wall or column bases. Low-pitched roof lines and exposed beams in overhanging eaves are also tell-tale characteristics. Inside, full second floors with bedrooms and game rooms are common, but so are sprawling single stories that take advantage of the low roofs for a more horizontal look. With unlimited square footage, you can have two walk-in closets in the master bedroom instead of only one, or give one to each of the family bedrooms. Add a window-side sitting room in the master suite or a sunroom near the kitchen. Make visiting friends and family feel welcome with a fully-equipped guest suite. The sky's the limit!

Just because you want to build a Craftsman-style home, it doesn't mean you're limited to a smaller square footage. Craftsman characteristics can be applied to any-sized structure, so have fun with it. On the outside, it can be a simple, earthy bungalow; on the inside, your own luxury estate. ∎

This cross-gable design features an innovative layout. The three-car garage is practical and attractive. Turn to page 153 to see more of plan HPK1800142.

A stunning shingle home with stone accents (including a stone fireplace!), this Cape Cod-style home will complement any neighborhood. Inside, the two-story foyer presents a grand staircase and high ceilings throughout. Multipane windows light up the living room and an archway connects it to the family room. Here, a lateral fireplace allows rear views. The breakfast nook has French doors to the rear property, inviting outdoor dining. The island kitchen is designed with lots of extra space to accommodate two cooks. A butler's pantry makes entertaining a breeze. Upstairs, three bedrooms (or make one a den) share a full bath and a bonus room. The master suite is graced with a vaulted ceiling and a private bath with a Roman spa tub.

plan# HPK1800107

Style: Cape Cod
First Floor: 1,319 sq. ft.
Second Floor: 1,181 sq. ft.
Total: 2,500 sq. ft.
Bonus Space: 371 sq. ft.
Bedrooms: 4
Bathrooms: 2½
Width: 60' - 0"
Depth: 42' - 0"
Foundation: Crawlspace

ORDER ONLINE @ EPLANS.COM

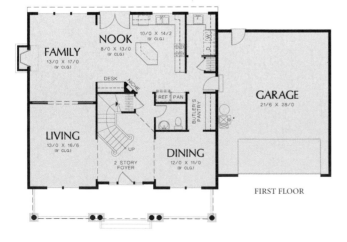

FIRST FLOOR

SECOND FLOOR

plan# HPK1800108

Style: Craftsman
First Floor: 1,799 sq. ft.
Second Floor: 709 sq. ft.
Total: 2,508 sq. ft.
Bonus Space: 384 sq. ft.
Bedrooms: 3
Bathrooms: 2½
Width: 77' - 4"
Depth: 41' - 4"
Foundation: Unfinished Walkout Basement

ORDER ONLINE @ EPLANS.COM

An oversized dormer above the entryway and a steep, side-gabled roof bring an interesting front perspective to this Craftsman-style vacation home. Inside, a wood-burning fireplace warms the family room, overlooked by the second-floor walkway. To the left, the master suite is attended by a large walk-in closet and double vanities in the bathroom. Owners will also appreciate the private access to the deck. The full-sized garage at the right of the plan features a bonus room on the upper floor.

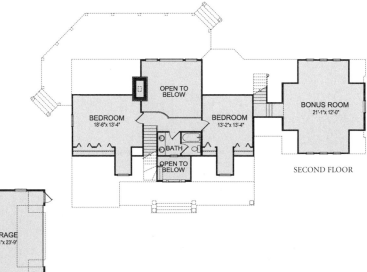

SECOND FLOOR

FIRST FLOOR

Three bedrooms, spacious family living areas, and plenty of amenities make this Craftsman design a pleasure to come home to. Vaulted ceilings enhance the den and living room, and built-in bookshelves, a media center, and a fireplace highlight the family room. The kitchen, with a built-in desk and island cooktop, serves the breakfast nook and dining room with ease. Sleeping quarters—the vaulted master suite and two family bedrooms— are upstairs, along with a bonus room and the utility area.

plan# HPK1800109

Style: Craftsman
First Floor: 1,360 sq. ft.
Second Floor: 1,154 sq. ft.
Total: 2,514 sq. ft.
Bonus Space: 202 sq. ft.
Bedrooms: 3
Bathrooms: 2½
Width: 52' - 0"
Depth: 45' - 6"
Foundation: Crawlspace

ORDER ONLINE @ EPLANS.COM

FIRST FLOOR

SECOND FLOOR

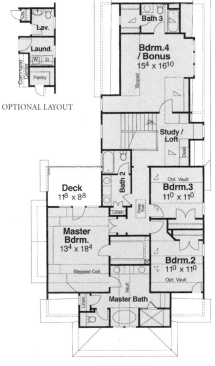

plan# HPK1800110

Style: Craftsman
First Floor: 1,294 sq. ft.
Second Floor: 1,220 sq. ft.
Total: 2,514 sq. ft.
Bonus Space: 366 sq. ft.
Bedrooms: 3
Bathrooms: 2½
Width: 38' - 0"
Depth: 76' - 0"
Foundation: Unfinished Walkout
Basement

ORDER ONLINE @ EPLANS.COM

The unassuming facade of this traditional home offers few clues about how ideal this design is for entertaining. The lack of unnecessary walls achieves a clean, smart layout that flows seamlessly. A side deck accessed from the living room and breakfast area extends the gathering outside. Upstairs houses all of the family bedrooms including the master suite, enhanced by a spacious private deck. Two additional family bedrooms share a full bath. A bonus fourth bedroom boasts a full bath and could be used as a recreation/exercise/guest room. The central study/loft area is perfect for a family computer.

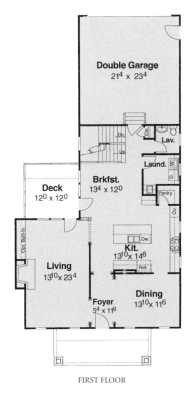

FIRST FLOOR

OPTIONAL LAYOUT

SECOND FLOOR

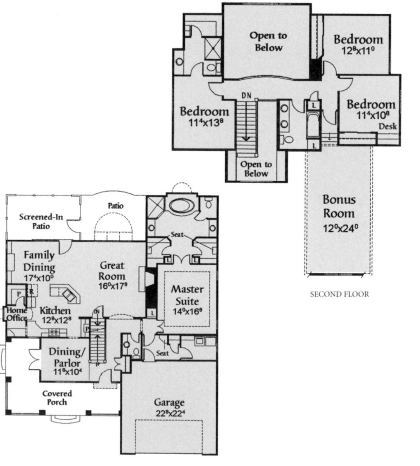

SECOND FLOOR

FIRST FLOOR

plan # HPK1800111

Style: Craftsman
First Floor: 1,711 sq. ft.
Second Floor: 805 sq. ft.
Total: 2,516 sq. ft.
Bedrooms: 4
Bathrooms: 3½
Width: 50' - 8"
Depth: 62' - 0"
Foundation: Unfinished Basement

ORDER ONLINE @ EPLANS.COM

Craftsman styling warms this country home, with its extensive covered porch that turns the corner with lots of charm and an invitation for outdoor living at its best. In a departure from cottage architecture of the past, the main-floor living spaces in this contemporary rendering of the bungalow are open and airy. A master bedroom suite allows empty-nesters to live on a single level, or parents a separate retreat that is still within hailing distance of the rooms upstairs. A balcony on the second floor overlooks the main living spaces and connects the three bedrooms. A laundry room off the two-car garage and a home office off the kitchen promise efficient work space out of the main stream of activity.

plan# HPK1800112

Style: Craftsman
First Floor: 1,862 sq. ft.
Second Floor: 661 sq. ft.
Total: 2,523 sq. ft.
Bonus Space: 315 sq. ft.
Bedrooms: 3
Bathrooms: 2½
Width: 56' - 0"
Depth: 56' - 6"
Foundation: Unfinished Walkout
Basement, Crawlspace

ORDER ONLINE @ EPLANS.COM

Fabulous amenities and breathtaking heights are exciting features of this traditional design. The huge vaulted family room with fireplace dominates the center of the plan, separating the master suite and dining/cooking areas. Upstairs, an overlook loft provides utility space as well as design interest for the upstairs bedrooms. An optional bonus room is an inspiring blank canvas for the owners to express their lifestyle; turn the space into a study, exercise room, home office, media room, studio, or fourth bedroom. Pleasing dormers and a gabled entry beautify the exterior.

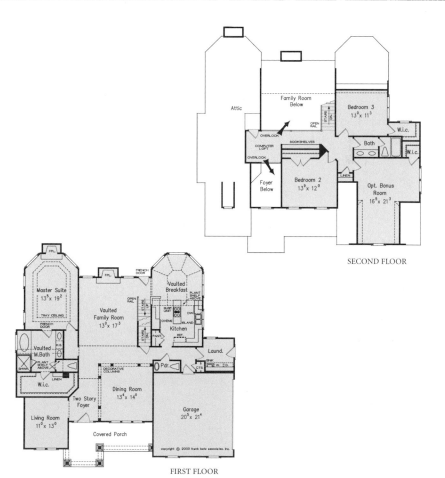

SECOND FLOOR

FIRST FLOOR

A brick and cedar exterior and wraparound porch decorate the front of this beautiful two-story home. An abundance of windows, stylish furniture alcoves and a wood-burning fireplace set this plan apart from the crowd. An island in the kitchen provides additional workspace and offers seating for quick meals. The master suite is topped with a vaulted ceiling and offers a whirlpool tub, dual vanities and a large walk-in closet. Three secondary bedrooms and a study loft reside on the upper level. A bonus room over the garage makes a great home office or studio.

plan # HPK1800113

Style: Craftsman
First Floor: 1,772 sq. ft.
Second Floor: 765 sq. ft.
Total: 2,537 sq. ft.
Bedrooms: 4
Bathrooms: 2½
Width: 61' - 8"
Depth: 66' - 4"
Foundation: Unfinished Basement

ORDER ONLINE @ EPLANS.COM

FIRST FLOOR

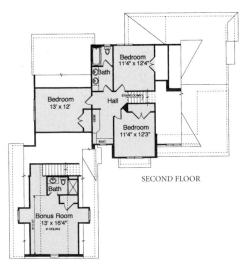

SECOND FLOOR

plan # HPK1800114

Style: Craftsman
Square Footage: 2,541
Bedrooms: 4
Bathrooms: 3
Width: 81' - 0"
Depth: 54' - 0"
Foundation: Unfinished Basement,
Slab, Crawlspace

ORDER ONLINE @ EPLANS.COM

This alluring Craftsman home includes decorative stone detailing, noble pillars, and enchanting windows. The covered porch leads into the gallery and just through the pillars is the great room, where the focal point falls on the fireplace. The kitchen features an island and a snack bar with a breakfast nook nearby. Easy access to the covered rear patio is made through the nook. A guest bedroom is located away from the family sleeping quarters for privacy. Two family bedrooms and a master suite comprise the left side of the plan.

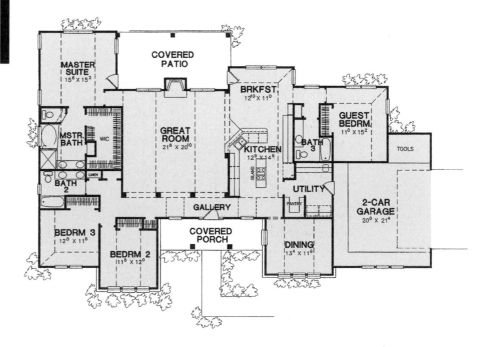

A combination of stone and siding add to the charm of this Craftsman home. Space is optimized with the gathering room, kitchen, and living room flowing together in one open area, yet each remaining distinct. The wall of windows and doors across the rear wall showcase the exterior view. The open area by the stairs on the second floor provides a dramatic view of the foyer below. The vaulted master suite enjoys a sizeable walk-in closet and a soothing bath and the windows offer a spectacular view from the tub. Plenty of storage space and a hobby room by the garage are added bonuses to this home that is sure to be the talk of the neighborhood.

plan # HPK1800115

Style: Craftsman
First Floor: 1,310 sq. ft.
Second Floor: 1,249 sq. ft.
Total: 2,559 sq. ft.
Bedrooms: 4
Bathrooms: 2½
Width: 45' - 0"
Depth: 47' - 0"
Foundation: Unfinished Basement

ORDER ONLINE @ EPLANS.COM

BASEMENT

FIRST FLOOR

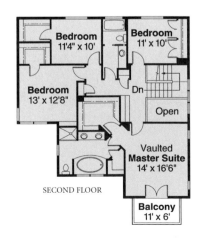

SECOND FLOOR

plan# HPK1800116

Style: Craftsman
First Floor: 1,322 sq. ft.
Second Floor: 1,262 sq. ft.
Total: 2,584 sq. ft.
Bedrooms: 4
Bathrooms: 3
Width: 48' - 0"
Depth: 50' - 0"
Foundation: Crawlspace, Unfinished
Walkout Basement, Slab

ORDER ONLINE @ EPLANS.COM

With Craftsman detail and traditional charm, this four-bedroom home captures the comfort and style you've been searching for. From a wrapping porch enter the two-story foyer with a decorative niche that displays special photos or treasures to all your guests. Continue to a beautiful family room, graced with a two-story ceiling and second-floor radius windows. The kitchen is open and spacious, leading to a breakfast area, hearth-warmed keeping room, and elegant dining room. A bedroom on this level also serves as an ideal den or home office. Upstairs, two secondary bedrooms share a full bath. The master suite is ready for relaxation with a sunny sitting room and soothing vaulted bath. A laundry room on this level makes wash day a breeze.

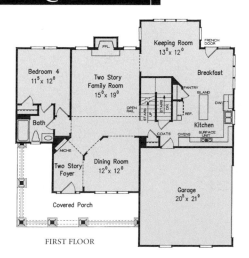

FIRST FLOOR

SECOND FLOOR

Little things mean a lot—and here, the details add up to a marvelous plan. Exterior elements lend curb appeal to the two-story layout. Stone accents, lap siding, and a dormer window highlight the attention in the exterior planning. Both formal and casual dining spaces are included and flank an open kitchen that overlooks the great room. At the back of the plan, near a service entry to the double garage, are a laundry room and half-bath. Sleeping quarters are upstairs, and include three family bedrooms and a master suite. A spa tub, separate shower, dual sinks, and a walk-in closet highlight the master bath. Family bedrooms share a full bath with double sinks.

plan # HPK1800117

Style: Craftsman
First Floor: 1,216 sq. ft.
Second Floor: 1,390 sq. ft.
Total: 2,606 sq. ft.
Bedrooms: 4
Bathrooms: 2½
Width: 50' - 0"
Depth: 42' - 0"
Foundation: Crawlspace

ORDER ONLINE @ EPLANS.COM

FIRST FLOOR

SECOND FLOOR

plan # HPK1800118

Style: Craftsman
First Floor: 1,755 sq. ft.
Second Floor: 864 sq. ft.
Total: 2,619 sq. ft.
Bedrooms: 4
Bathrooms: 3½
Width: 56' - 0"
Depth: 53' - 0"
Foundation: Crawlspace, Unfinished
Walkout Basement, Slab

ORDER ONLINE @ EPLANS.COM

Open-face gables, broad white trim, and double-hung window sashes create appeal on this cottage's exterior. Inside, a comfortable and modern design of the great room caters to the active family requiring more functional than formal space. The island kitchen will be a favorite hangout. A formal dining room is perfect for entertaining and hosting holiday meals. A first-floor master suite includes an amenity-filled bath and imperial-sized walk-in closet. Upstairs, three secondary bedrooms share two full baths.

SECOND FLOOR

FIRST FLOOR

True Craftsman styling marks the exterior of this house; the low-pitched gable roof and expansive, columned front porch are characteristic of this style. Once inside, the floor plan fits the ideal for an average-sized family. Four bedrooms and three baths are enhanced with living spaces to be admired. On the first floor is a spacious island kitchen with a serving bar to the adjacent rear-facing vaulted breakfast nook, bathed in light from a bevy of windows. A bedroom and full bath, a dining room set off by decorative columns, and a hearth-warmed two-story family room round out this level. Wash day is a breeze with the second-story laundry room that caters to the three bedrooms and two full baths upstairs.

plan # HPK1800119

Style: Craftsman
First Floor: 1,464 sq. ft.
Second Floor: 1,164 sq. ft.
Total: 2,628 sq. ft.
Bedrooms: 4
Bathrooms: 3
Width: 55' - 4"
Depth: 55' - 0"
Foundation: Unfinished Walkout Basement, Crawlspace

ORDER ONLINE @ EPLANS.COM

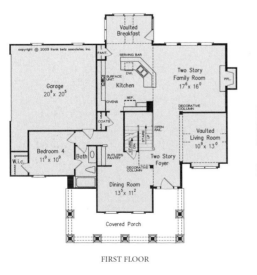

FIRST FLOOR

SECOND FLOOR

REAR EXTERIOR

A mixture of exterior materials enhances the curb appeal of this hillside home, while a large deck, screened porch, and patio promote outdoor living. With the rear wall comprised of windows and French doors, both levels receive an abundance of natural light and take advantage of views. A cathedral ceiling with exposed beams crowns the kitchen and great room, creating voluminous spaces. Built-in cabinetry, a versatile study/bedroom, sizable utility room, and home office all add convenience. The master suite is complete with a tray ceiling in the bedroom, French door leading to the screened porch, dual walk-in closets, and an exquisite bath.

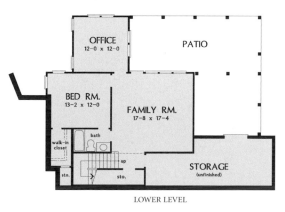

LOWER LEVEL

MAIN LEVEL

Centered windows on front-facing gables perch atop a Craftsman-style porch, creating a delightful neighborhood home. The uncluttered layout takes full advantage of the casual living areas. A vaulted family room features a fireplace with sidelights and an uninterrupted perspective of the breakfast space and island kitchen. Enjoy alfresco dining on the screened porch. The first-floor master suite is enhanced by a tray ceiling and super bath. Across the hall, a home office gazes upon the front yard. Additional bedrooms are placed on the second level, each sporting a walk-in closet and having access to the vaulted loft area.

plan# HPK1800121

Style: Craftsman
First Floor: 1,845 sq. ft.
Second Floor: 799 sq. ft.
Total: 2,644 sq. ft.
Bedrooms: 4
Bathrooms: 3
Width: 61' - 0"
Depth: 57' - 4"
Foundation: Crawlspace, Unfinished Walkout Basement, Slab

ORDER ONLINE @ EPLANS.COM

FIRST FLOOR

SECOND FLOOR

plan # HPK1800122

Style: Craftsman
First Floor: 1,650 sq. ft.
Second Floor: 1,038 sq. ft.
Total: 2,688 sq. ft.
Bedrooms: 4
Bathrooms: 3½
Width: 50' - 0"
Depth: 60' - 0"

ORDER ONLINE @ EPLANS.COM

Charming highlights abound in this quaint family manor. A petite covered porch welcomes you to the foyer; inside, the dining room/optional study is open to the immense living room with a corner fireplace. The kitchen features an island, pantry, and an eating bar which overlooks the bayed breakfast nook. The three-car garage accommodates everyone in the family. The master suite resides on the first floor for privacy and offers a private bath and walk-in closet. Upstairs, three family bedrooms and a playroom complete the home.

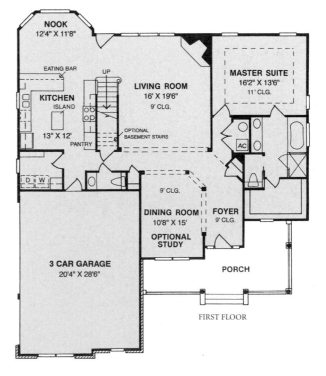

FIRST FLOOR

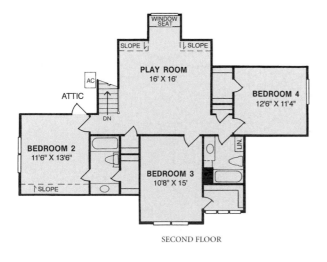

SECOND FLOOR

This plan says "welcome home," as Craftsman details make a warm entry. The view from the front door to the family room's two-story fireplace wall is amazing. The garage entry brings you past a home office that can easily be used as a guest bedroom. The expansive kitchen/breakfast area also features a command center—perfect for the family computer. A staircase leads to the second-floor balcony where three bedrooms share a bath. The master suite features a window seat on the back wall, dramatized by a stepped ceiling and large windows overlooking the back yard. An oversized master closet even has extra storage space that could be cedar-lined for those out-of-season clothes. The second-floor laundry and computer desk complete this well-appointed design.

plan# HPK1800123

Style: Craftsman
First Floor: 1,315 sq. ft.
Second Floor: 1,380 sq. ft.
Total: 2,695 sq. ft.
Bedrooms: 5
Bathrooms: 3
Width: 50' - 0"
Depth: 44' - 0"
Foundation: Unfinished Walkout Basement

ORDER ONLINE @ EPLANS.COM

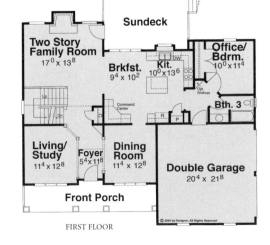

FIRST FLOOR

SECOND FLOOR

plan# HPK1800124

Style: Bungalow
First Floor: 1,798 sq. ft.
Second Floor: 900 sq. ft.
Total: 2,698 sq. ft.
Bedrooms: 3
Bathrooms: 3½
Width: 54' - 0"
Depth: 57' - 0"
Foundation: Crawlspace

ORDER ONLINE @ EPLANS.COM

This rustic stone-and-siding exterior with Craftsman influences includes a multitude of windows flooding the interior with natural light. The foyer opens to the great room, which is complete with three sets of French doors and a two-sided fireplace. The master suite offers an expansive private bath, two large walk-in closets, a bay window, and a tray ceiling. The dining room, kitchen, and utility room make an efficient trio.

SECOND FLOOR

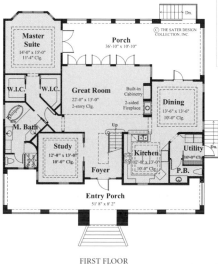

FIRST FLOOR

Stylish windows and rooflines on the exterior and elegant arches inside reflect the designer's goal of giving you a good-looking, comfortable home. From the two-story foyer enter the formal living and dining rooms through wide, arched entries. Straight ahead another arched entry takes you into the family room. The family room, breakfast area, and kitchen are a trio running along the entire rear of the plan; a classy arch marks the line between the family room and the others. Upstairs, the bright and airy master suite enjoys a vaulted sitting area and private access to a covered porch. Three more bedrooms, a bath, and a convenient laundry are also situated on this floor. The two-car garage can be accessed from either the kitchen or the dining room.

plan# HPK1800125

Style: Craftsman
First Floor: 1,249 sq. ft.
Second Floor: 1,458 sq. ft.
Total: 2,707 sq. ft.
Bedrooms: 4
Bathrooms: 2½
Width: 57' - 4"
Depth: 39' - 0"
Foundation: Crawlspace, Unfinished Walkout Basement

ORDER ONLINE @ EPLANS.COM

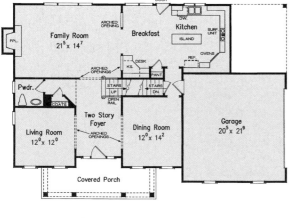

FIRST FLOOR

SECOND FLOOR

plan # HPK1800126

Style: Craftsman
First Floor: 1,243 sq. ft.
Second Floor: 1,474 sq. ft.
Total: 2,717 sq. ft.
Bedrooms: 4
Bathrooms: 3½
Width: 46' - 4"
Depth: 66' - 0"
Foundation: Crawlspace, Unfinished
Walkout Basement

ORDER ONLINE @ EPLANS.COM

There's an old-fashioned, settled-in feel about this two-story home with a hint of Craftsman styling. The inviting front porch will bring hours of quiet relaxation. An impressive barrel-vault ceiling highlights the hallway that opens to a coat closet and half-bath and leads to both a stairway and the spacious family room. The breakfast alcove is marked off from the kitchen by an angled serving bar. Upstairs, the absolutely modern master suite enjoys separate sitting and sleeping areas, each with a tray ceiling; French doors lead into the amenity-packed bath. Under a vaulted ceiling, a garden bath, shower, and two vanities will bring soothing relaxation; a radius window artfully draws in natural light. Tucked in a rear corner of the first floor is a laundry that can be entered either from the breakfast/kitchen area or from outside through a small rear covered porch.

SECOND FLOOR

FIRST FLOOR

Soaring ceilings help accent the spaciousness of this impressive two-story design that reveals a touch of Craftsman style. Two fireplaces—one in the vaulted keeping room, the other flanked by radius transoms in the family room—create a cozy atmosphere. The centrally positioned kitchen enjoys an island counter, serving bar, loads of counter space, and, best of all, a walk-in pantry. The entire left wing embraces the resplendent master suite; upstairs, three more bedrooms, all with walk-in closets, offer ample sleeping space for children or guests. Two baths and space for future development are also located on this floor.

plan # HPK1800127

Style: Craftsman
First Floor: 1,909 sq. ft.
Second Floor: 835 sq. ft.
Total: 2,744 sq. ft.
Bonus Space: 165 sq. ft.
Bedrooms: 4
Bathrooms: 3½
Width: 56' - 0"
Depth: 51' - 4"
Foundation: Crawlspace, Unfinished Walkout Basement

ORDER ONLINE @ EPLANS.COM

FIRST FLOOR

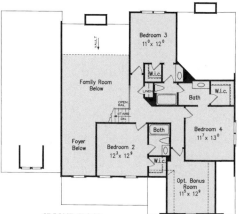

SECOND FLOOR

ORDER BLUEPRINTS 24 HOURS, 7 DAYS A WEEK, AT 1-800-521-6797

plan# HPK1800128

Style: Bungalow
First Floor: 1,855 sq. ft.
Second Floor: 901 sq. ft.
Total: 2,756 sq. ft.
Bedrooms: 3
Bathrooms: 3½
Width: 66' - 0"
Depth: 50' - 0"
Foundation: Unfinished Walkout Basement

ORDER ONLINE @ EPLANS.COM

This luxurious vacation cabin is the perfect rustic paradise, whether set by a lake or a mountain scene. The wraparound entry porch is friendly and inviting. Double doors open into the foyer, that is flanked on either side by the study—with built-in cabinetry—and the formal dining room. The octagonal great room features a vaulted ceiling, a fireplace, and a built-in entertainment center. The gourmet island kitchen is brightened by a bayed window and a pass-through to the lanai. A set of private double doors opens to the vaulted master lanai. Two family bedrooms with private baths are featured upstairs. A computer center, a morning kitchen, and a second-floor deck are located at the end of the hall.

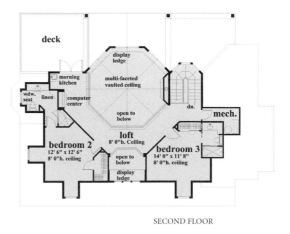

SECOND FLOOR

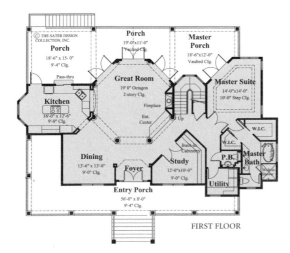

FIRST FLOOR

FIRST FLOOR

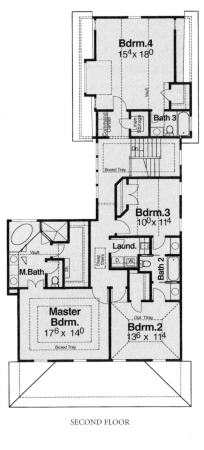

SECOND FLOOR

plan# HPK1800129

Style: Prairie
First Floor: 1,198 sq. ft.
Second Floor: 1,570 sq. ft.
Total: 2,768 sq. ft.
Bedrooms: 4
Bathrooms: 3½
Width: 38' - 0"
Depth: 75' - 0"
Foundation: Crawlspace

ORDER ONLINE @ EPLANS.COM

Ideal for a narrow city lot, this urban in-fill home is a city- dweller's dream. The open first-floor layout offers easy inter-action between rooms. Access to a rear deck from the living room and breakfast area makes outdoor dining a possibility. The sleeping quarters are housed upstairs, including the master suite and three addi-tional family bedrooms. Bedroom 4 boasts a private, full bath; nearby are a linen storage closet and the command center control panel for the home automation system. The second-floor laundry room is an added con-venience.

plan # HPK1800130

Style: Bungalow
First Floor: 1,706 sq. ft.
Second Floor: 1,123 sq. ft.
Total: 2,829 sq. ft.
Bedrooms: 3
Bathrooms: 2½
Width: 71' - 2"
Depth: 64' - 6"
Foundation: Crawlspace

ORDER ONLINE @ EPLANS.COM

Plentiful outdoor living spaces make this an ideal home for entertaining. Inside, the open floor plan allows easy interaction between rooms. The spacious island kitchen conveniently serves the family room and dining room. At the rear of the first floor, a fireplace warms the living room. Upstairs houses the master bedroom, outfitted with tray ceilings, a dual-sink vanity, a garden tub and separate shower, and a compartmented toilet. The adjacent home office is an added convenience. Two additional family bedrooms share a full bath. A three-car garage completes this plan.

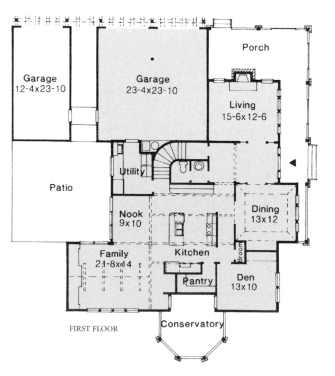

FIRST FLOOR

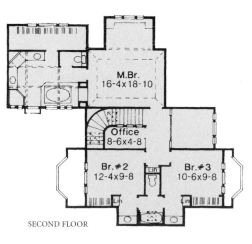

SECOND FLOOR

A two-story Craftsman with a bevy of amenities, this home is sure to please. The two-story foyer is flanked by the formal living room and dining room, and leads into the spacious family room. A fireplace in the family room adds warmth to the space. A serving bar in the kitchen allows for casual meals and easy interaction between the breakfast area and family room. The master suite and three additional bedrooms are housed upstairs. The master suite, enhanced by a tray ceiling, boasts a private sitting room with window seat, a huge walk-in closet, a roomy bath with dual-sink vanities, a separate shower and tub, and a private toilet.

plan # HPK1800131

Style: Craftsman
First Floor: 1,367 sq. ft.
Second Floor: 1,492 sq. ft.
Total: 2,859 sq. ft.
Bedrooms: 4
Bathrooms: 2½
Width: 58' - 0"
Depth: 45' - 0"
Foundation: Crawlspace, Unfinished Walkout Basement

ORDER ONLINE @ EPLANS.COM

FIRST FLOOR

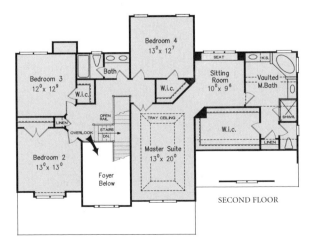

SECOND FLOOR

plan# HPK1800132

Style: Prairie
First Floor: 1,440 sq. ft.
Second Floor: 1,440 sq. ft.
Total: 2,880 sq. ft.
Bonus Space: 140 sq. ft.
Bedrooms: 4
Bathrooms: 2½
Width: 30' - 0"
Depth: 56' - 0"
Foundation: Unfinished Basement

ORDER ONLINE @ EPLANS.COM

The impressive exterior gives way to an interior without boundaries. The lack of unnecessary walls creates a feeling of spaciousness. Access to the sundeck from the family room extends the living space, encouraging entertaining. The second floor houses the master suite and three additional family bedrooms. Bedrooms 2 and 3 enjoy private access to a front-facing covered porch. A second-floor laundry room is an added convenience. The finished basement, boasting a sizable recreation room, completes this plan.

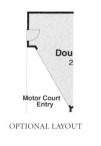

Dou
2

Motor Court
Entry

OPTIONAL LAYOUT

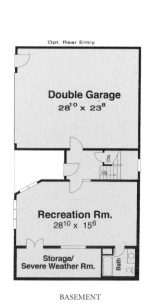

Sitting
12⁴ x 11⁴

Lnd.

OPTIONAL LAYOUT

Opt. Rear Entry

Double Garage
28¹⁰ x 23⁸

Up

Recreation Rm.
28¹⁰ x 15⁶

Storage/
Severe Weather Rm.

Bath

BASEMENT

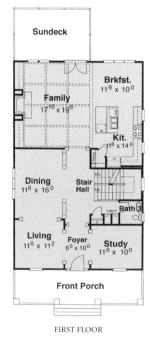

Sundeck

Brkfst.
11⁶ x 10⁰

Family
17¹⁰ x 19⁶

Kit.
11⁶ x 14⁰

Dining
11⁶ x 16⁰

Stair
Hall

Up

Bath 3

Living
11⁶ x 11²

Foyer
6⁰ x 10⁰

Study
11⁶ x 10⁰

Front Porch

FIRST FLOOR

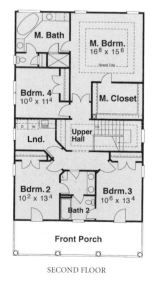

M. Bath

M. Bdrm.
16⁸ x 15⁶

Bdrm. 4
10⁰ x 11⁴

M. Closet

Lnd.

Upper
Hall

Bdrm. 2
10² x 13⁴

Bath 2

Bdrm. 3
10⁶ x 13⁴

Front Porch

SECOND FLOOR

The strong impact of its exterior design will make this home look good in the country or the suburbs. Upon entering, guests are greeted with the expansive great room's cathedral ceiling and cozy fireplace. The kitchen has a snack-counter island with a breakfast nook that opens to a deck. Located on the first floor for privacy, the master suite contains plenty of windows, two walk-in closets, and a whirlpool tub with views out a bayed window. The immaculate second floor overlooks the great room and entryway. A lounge area is flanked by Bedrooms 2 and 3. A full bath with dual vanities completes the plan.

plan # HPK1800133

Style: Bungalow
First Floor: 2,078 sq. ft.
Second Floor: 823 sq. ft.
Total: 2,901 sq. ft.
Bedrooms: 3
Bathrooms: 2½
Width: 88' - 5"
Depth: 58' - 3"
Foundation: Unfinished Basement

ORDER ONLINE @ EPLANS.COM

FIRST FLOOR

SECOND FLOOR

plan # HPK1800134

Style: Craftsman
First Floor: 1,335 sq. ft.
Second Floor: 1,572 sq. ft.
Total: 2,907 sq. ft.
Bedrooms: 4
Bathrooms: 3½
Width: 55' - 0"
Depth: 45' - 0"
Foundation: Crawlspace, Unfinished
Walkout Basement

ORDER ONLINE @ EPLANS.COM

Brick pillars line the front porch of this vintage-style country home and flower-box windows add undeniable charm. Inside, the two-story foyer opens on either side to formal rooms, adorned with columns. A touch of elegance graces the family room, where a coffered ceiling and built-in framed fireplace create a welcoming atmosphere. Opening to the breakfast bay is the island kitchen, enjoying a plentiful pantry. Three secondary bedrooms on the upper level provide space for family and guests, including a generous suite. The master suite soothes with a vaulted sitting area and bath, and a walk-in closet with more than ample storage. A laundry room is located on this level for extra convenience.

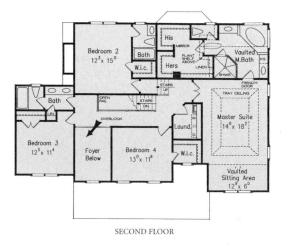

SECOND FLOOR

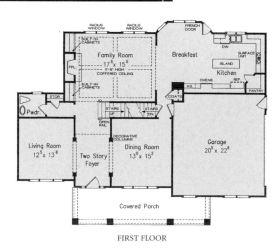

FIRST FLOOR

© 1999 Donald A. Gardner, Inc.

A stunning center dormer with an arched window embellishes the exterior of this Craftsman-style home. The dormer's arched window allows light into the foyer and built-in niche. The second-floor hall is a balcony that overlooks both the foyer and great room. A generous back porch extends the great room, which features an impressive vaulted ceiling and fireplace; a tray ceiling adorns the formal dining room. The master suite, which includes a tray ceiling as well, enjoys back-porch access, a built-in cabinet, generous walk-in closet, and private bath. Two more bedrooms are located upstairs; a fourth can be found in the basement, along with a family room.

plan# HPK1800135

Style: Craftsman
Main Level: 1,662 sq. ft.
Upper Level: 585 sq. ft.
Lower Level: 706 sq. ft.
Total: 2,953 sq. ft.
Bonus Space: 575 sq. ft.
Bedrooms: 4
Bathrooms: 3½
Width: 81' - 4"
Depth: 68' - 8"

ORDER ONLINE @ EPLANS.COM

LOWER LEVEL

REAR EXTERIOR

MAIN LEVEL

UPPER LEVEL

plan# HPK1800136

Style: Craftsman
First Floor: 1,440 sq. ft.
Second Floor: 1,514 sq. ft.
Total: 2,954 sq. ft.
Bedrooms: 4
Bathrooms: 3½
Width: 30' - 0"
Depth: 68' - 0"
Foundation: Unfinished Walkout
Basement

ORDER ONLINE @ EPLANS.COM

A stylish Craftsman at just under 3,000 square feet, this home features an open layout ideal for entertaining. Rooms are distinguished by columns, eliminating the use of unnecessary walls. At the rear of the home, the expansive family room, warmed by a fireplace, faces the adjoining breakfast area and kitchen. Access to the sundeck makes alfresco meals an option. A walk-in pantry is an added bonus. The second floor houses the family bedrooms, including the lavish master suite; two bedrooms separated by a Jack-and-Jill bath; and a fourth bedroom with a private, full bath. The second-floor laundry room is smart and convenient. A centrally located, optional computer station is perfect for a family computer. A sizable recreation room on the basement level completes this plan.

OPTIONAL LAYOUT

OPTIONAL LAYOUT

BASEMENT

SECOND FLOOR

FIRST FLOOR

This delightful vacation home, designed for relaxation, will fit as well on a lakefront as in the mountains. Rear and front covered porches help to extend the living space outdoors. Three upstairs bedrooms, with an option for a fourth, offer plenty of room to put up family members and guests. A possible media room or office on the same level allows space to get some work done at home. On the main level, a luxurious master suite, informal living room, formal dining room, and a grand room with an extended hearth fireplace are located. The hub of family activity will be the area that includes the keeping room with a cozy fireplace, breakfast nook, and magnificent kitchen where an island counter will make food preparation a breeze.

plan # HPK1800137

Style: Craftsman
First Floor: 2,160 sq. ft.
Second Floor: 828 sq. ft.
Total: 2,988 sq. ft.
Bonus Space: 541 sq. ft.
Bedrooms: 4
Bathrooms: 3½
Width: 68' - 3"
Depth: 60' - 11"
Foundation: Unfinished Walkout Basement

ORDER ONLINE @ EPLANS.COM

FIRST FLOOR

SECOND FLOOR

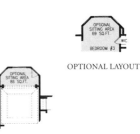

OPTIONAL LAYOUT

OPTIONAL LAYOUT

plan# HPK1800138

Style: Craftsman
First Floor: 2,172 sq. ft.
Second Floor: 824 sq. ft.
Total: 2,996 sq. ft.
Bedrooms: 3
Bathrooms: 2½
Width: 67' - 0"
Depth: 68' - 0"
Foundation: Crawlspace

ORDER ONLINE @ EPLANS.COM

REAR EXTERIOR

Arts and Crafts style has never looked so appealing! A steeply pitched front gable accented with cedar shingles and stone is set-off by gentle porch arches. Inside, find the desirable great room/kitchen combination with an adjacent breakfast nook. A first-floor master suite offers a walk-in closet, compartmented bath, and decorative ceiling. Conveniently placed, the den functions as a perfect office or library. Two family bedrooms, a gallery library, and the game room share a spacious hall bath.

SECOND FLOOR

FIRST FLOOR

A picture-perfect addition to any neighborhood, this Craftsman home is brimming with curb appeal. Inside, the imaginative design is abound with amenities. Highlights include intricate ceiling treatments, built-in bookcases and desks, and plant shelves. The island kitchen is open to the family room, enabling constant interaction. Access to a rear patio invites the option of alfresco meals. The second floor houses four bedrooms, including the master suite. The fourth bedroom can be used as an office or a guest suite. Extra storage space in the two-car garage is an added bonus.

plan # HPK1800139

Style: Craftsman
First Floor: 1,285 sq. ft.
Second Floor: 1,726 sq. ft.
Total: 3,011 sq. ft.
Bedrooms: 4
Bathrooms: 3½
Width: 44' - 0"
Depth: 50' - 0"
Foundation: Unfinished Walkout Basement

ORDER ONLINE @ EPLANS.COM

SIDE EXTERIOR

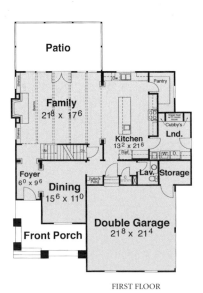

FIRST FLOOR

SECOND FLOOR

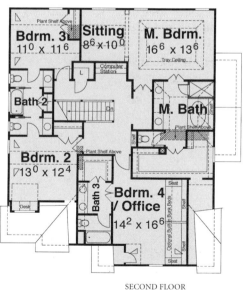

SECOND FLOOR

plan# HPK1800140

Style: Craftsman
First Floor: 1,285 sq. ft.
Second Floor: 1,726 sq. ft.
Total: 3,011 sq. ft.
Bedrooms: 4
Bathrooms: 3½
Width: 44' - 0"
Depth: 50' - 0"
Foundation: Unfinished Walkout Basement

ORDER ONLINE @ EPLANS.COM

Indulge in luxury Craftsman style. At just over 3,000 square feet this two-story home offers a wealth of amenities on each floor. The first floor boasts built-in shelves, a large island in the kitchen, a huge walk-in pantry, and a fireplace in the spacious family room. Upstairs, the master bedroom—enhanced by a tray ceiling—features a sitting room and a voluminous walk-in closet. The secondary bedrooms include additional built-ins. The centrally-located computer station is ideal for parental supervision.

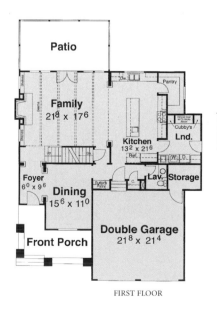

FIRST FLOOR

© Stephen Fuller, Inc.

This lovely Craftsman-style home invites enjoyment of the outdoors with a front covered porch and a spacious rear terrace. Inside, formal rooms flank the foyer and feature lovely amenities, such as French-door access to the front porch. A fireplace warms the family room, which provides plenty of natural light and wide views through three sets of glass doors. The first-floor master suite features a large walk-in closet, sumptuous bath, and plenty of windows. Additional bedrooms on the second floor enjoy a balcony overlook to the family room.

plan# HPK1800141

Style: Craftsman
First Floor: 1,924 sq. ft.
Second Floor: 1,097 sq. ft.
Total: 3,021 sq. ft.
Bonus Space: 352 sq. ft.
Bedrooms: 3
Bathrooms: 2½
Width: 68' - 3"
Depth: 53' - 0"
Foundation: Crawlspace

ORDER ONLINE @ EPLANS.COM

FIRST FLOOR

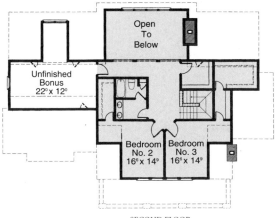

SECOND FLOOR

plan# HPK1800142

Style: Craftsman
Main Level: 1,268 sq. ft.
Upper Level: 931 sq. ft.
Lower Level: 949 sq. ft.
Total: 3,148 sq. ft.
Bedrooms: 4
Bathrooms: 3½
Width: 53' - 6"
Depth: 73' - 0"
Foundation: Finished Walkout Basement

ORDER ONLINE @ EPLANS.COM

A covered front porch provides a welcoming entry for this Craftsman design, which features a stunning, amenity-filled interior. Vaulted ceilings adorn the great room, office, and even the garage; the dining room includes a built-in hutch, and the kitchen boasts a walk-in pantry. Upstairs, the master suite offers a walk-in closet with built-in shelves, along with a private bath that contains a spa tub; two additional bedrooms also have walk-in closets. A fourth bedroom, a recreation room with a fireplace and wet bar, and a wine cellar reside on the lower level.

UPPER LEVEL

MAIN LEVEL

LOWER LEVEL

Varied and intriguing rooflines create an impressive and attractive design scale. The main level features a den with double French doors and front porch views. A nearby bedroom with private bath and walk-in closet can be used as a guest suite. Entertaining is a snap in the kitchen, dining room, and great room combination. Upstairs, two bedrooms share a hall bath. An open study is a great spot for a computer media center. The master suite features a large walk-in closet, roomy bath, and a private terrace. Expansion space can be completed later.

plan# HPK1800143

Style: Craftsman
First Floor: 1,846 sq. ft.
Second Floor: 1,309 sq. ft.
Total: 3,155 sq. ft.
Bonus Space: 563 sq. ft.
Bedrooms: 4
Bathrooms: 3½
Width: 77' - 6"
Depth: 48' - 8"
Foundation: Crawlspace

ORDER ONLINE @ EPLANS.COM

FIRST FLOOR

SECOND FLOOR

plan # HPK1800144

Style: Prairie
First Floor: 1,379 sq. ft.
Second Floor: 1,794 sq. ft.
Total: 3,173 sq. ft.
Bedrooms: 4
Bathrooms: 3½
Width: 38' - 0"
Depth: 80' - 0"
Foundation: Unfinished Walkout Basement

ORDER ONLINE @ EPLANS.COM

Bold columns distinguish the covered porch on this traditional home. Inside, the minimal use of walls is refreshing and opens the floor plan by adjoining living spaces. Access to the rear patio from the breakfast area makes alfresco meals a possibility. The second floor houses the spacious master suite, enhanced by a tray ceiling and private balcony. Two adjacent family bedrooms are separated by a Jack-and-Jill bath. A short hallway leads to the second-floor laundry room. The family computer station sits outside of bedroom 4—equipped with a full, private bath—useful as an ideal guest suite.

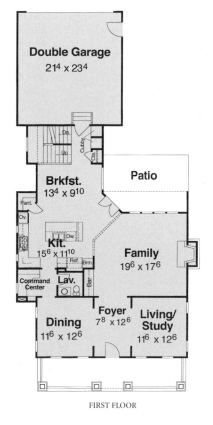

FIRST FLOOR

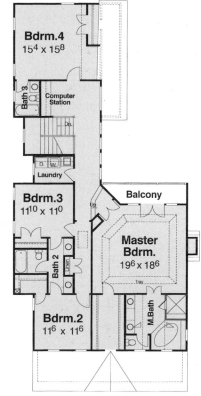

SECOND FLOOR

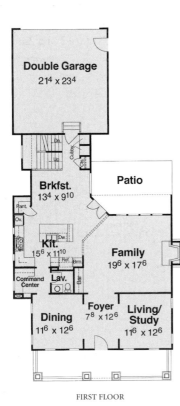

FIRST FLOOR

Double Garage
21⁴ x 23⁴

Brkfst.
13⁴ x 9¹⁰

Patio

Pant.

Kit
15⁶ x 11¹⁰

Family
19⁶ x 17⁶

Command Center

Lav.

Foyer
7⁸ x 12⁶

Living/Study
11⁶ x 12⁶

Dining
11⁶ x 12⁶

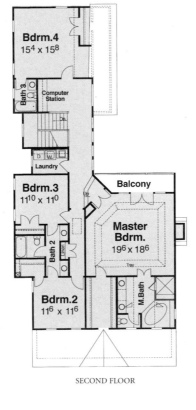

SECOND FLOOR

Bdrm.4
15⁴ x 15⁸

Bath 3

Computer Station

Laundry

Bdrm.3
11¹⁰ x 11⁰

Balcony

Bath 2

Linen

Master Bdrm.
19⁶ x 18⁶

Tray

Bdrm.2
11⁶ x 11⁶

M.Bath

plan # HPK1800145

Style: Prairie
First Floor: 1,379 sq. ft.
Second Floor: 1,794 sq. ft.
Total: 3,173 sq. ft.
Bedrooms: 4
Bathrooms: 3½
Width: 38' - 0"
Depth: 80' - 0"
Foundation: Unfinished Basement

ORDER ONLINE @ EPLANS.COM

A series of tapering columns anchored with brick, a wide covered porch, and deep eaves are Craftsman-style trademarks. The foyer is flanked by more formal spaces. To the back of the plan, the family room offers a deck view and fireplace. The kitchen is outfitted with a large island and convenient breakfast nook. The second floor is home to three family bedrooms—one with a private bath—and a computer station. The master suite opens through double doors and enjoys a private balcony, walk-in closet, and super bath.

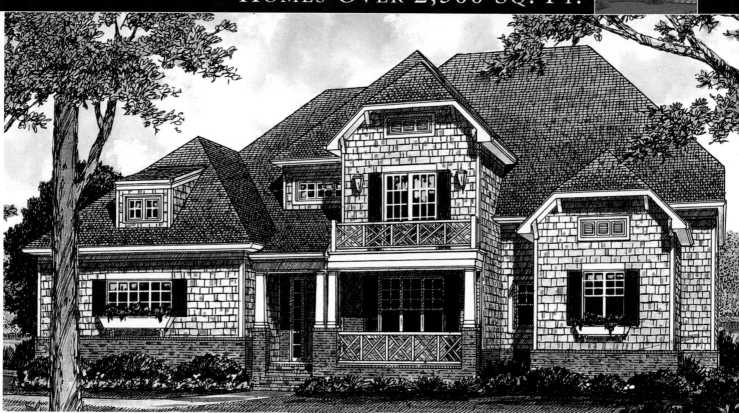

plan# HPK1800146

Style: Craftsman
First Floor: 1,890 sq. ft.
Second Floor: 1,286 sq. ft.
Total: 3,176 sq. ft.
Bonus Space: 431 sq. ft.
Bedrooms: 4
Bathrooms: 3½
Width: 67' - 0"
Depth: 56' - 8"
Foundation: Unfinished Basement

ORDER ONLINE @ EPLANS.COM

A mixture of rooflines gives this shingle-style home a unique look. Enter through the covered porch and to the right find the tray-ceilinged dining room. The great room—complete with a fireplace—is positioned at the rear of the house, away from street noise, and is granted backyard views through a set of windows. The kitchen is enhanced with a cooktop island, plenty of counter space, and a nearby bayed breakfast nook and powder room. The first-floor master suite is situated at the back of the house for maximum privacy and boasts His and Hers walk-in closets, a bay window, and many other amenities. The second level is home to three additional family suites—one with a balcony and the other two with bay windows—two full baths, and a bonus room.

FIRST FLOOR

SECOND FLOOR

© 1999 Donald A. Gardner, Inc.

A prominent center gable with an arched window accents the facade of this custom Craftsman home, which features an exterior of cedar shakes, siding, and stone. An open floor plan with generously proportioned rooms contributes to the spacious and relaxed atmosphere. The vaulted great room boasts a rear wall of windows, a fireplace bordered by built-in cabinets, and convenient access to the kitchen. A second-floor loft overlooks the great room for added drama. The master suite is completely secluded and enjoys a cathedral ceiling, back-porch access, a large walk-in closet, and a luxurious bath. The home includes three additional bedrooms and baths as well as a vaulted loft/study and a bonus room.

plan # HPK1800147

Style: Craftsman
First Floor: 2,477 sq. ft.
Second Floor: 742 sq. ft.
Total: 3,219 sq. ft.
Bonus Space: 419 sq. ft.
Bedrooms: 4
Bathrooms: 4
Width: 100' - 0"
Depth: 66' - 2"

ORDER ONLINE @ EPLANS.COM

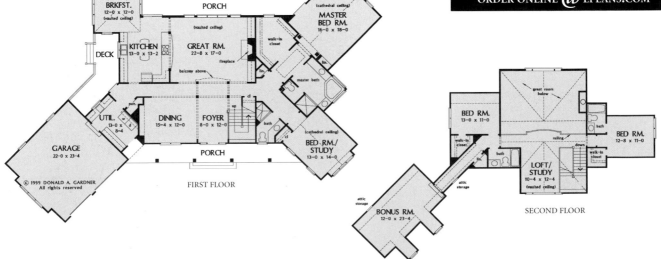

plan# HPK1800148

Style: Craftsman
First Floor: 1,388 sq. ft.
Second Floor: 1,835 sq. ft.
Total: 3,223 sq. ft.
Bedrooms: 4
Bathrooms: 3½
Width: 37' - 6"
Depth: 78' - 5"
Foundation: Unfinished Walkout Basement

ORDER ONLINE @ EPLANS.COM

Brick and siding blend seamlessly to inspire abundant curb appeal in this Craftsman home. Inside, the layout is equally seamless, incorporating a smart design. The kitchen easily serves the adjoining keeping room and breakfast nook. The screen porch and patio are ideal for entertaining and alfresco meals. Upstairs, the master suite, enhanced by stepped ceilings, boasts a lavish master bath and a private sitting area. Two additional family bedrooms are separated by a Jack-and-Jill bath. A computer station is conveniently located on this level. An exercise/media/guest room completes this plan.

SIDE EXTERIOR

FIRST FLOOR

SECOND FLOOR

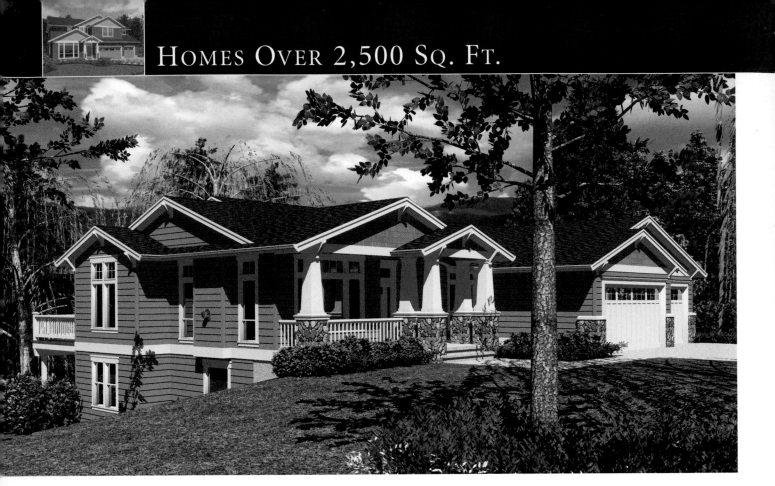

Perfect for a sloping lot, this Craftsman design boasts two levels of living space. Plenty of special amenities—vaulted ceilings in the living, dining, and family rooms, as well as in the master bedroom; built-ins in the family room and den; a large island cooktop in the kitchen; and an expansive rear deck—make this plan stand out. All three of the bedrooms—a main-level master suite and two lower-level bedrooms—include walk-in closets. Also on the lower level, find a recreation room with built-ins and a fireplace.

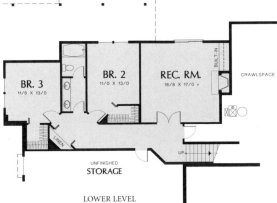

plan# HPK1800149

Style: Craftsman
Main Level: 2,170 sq. ft.
Lower Level: 1,076 sq. ft.
Total: 3,246 sq. ft.
Bedrooms: 3
Bathrooms: 2½
Width: 74' - 0"
Depth: 54' - 0"
Foundation: Slab, Walkout Basement

ORDER ONLINE @ EPLANS.COM

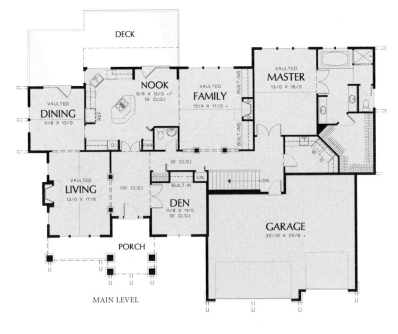

plan# HPK1800150

Style: Craftsman
First Floor: 1,649 sq. ft.
Second Floor: 1,604 sq. ft.
Total: 3,253 sq. ft.
Bedrooms: 4
Bathrooms: 3½
Width: 54' - 0"
Depth: 45' - 8"
Foundation: Slab, Unfinished
Walkout Basement

ORDER ONLINE @ EPLANS.COM

Coastal living at its finest, this home wears cedar shingles and siding with perfection. Front and rear porches extend living space for the family that loves the outdoors. Entertain on the weekend with well-designed formal spaces that flank the foyer. An open gallery hall transitions to the relaxed grand room featuring a fireplace and a wall of windows. Stairs to the second floor are to the rear. A spacious breakfast room offers lounging opportunity for guests to keep the cook company in the nearby fantastic island kitchen. Upstairs, large bedrooms give the family plenty of elbow room. A study loft is a great place for homework and an Internet connection. Framed by double doors, the master suite has everything. A private bath features dual-sink vanity, separate tub and shower, compartmented toilet, and oversized walk-in closet.

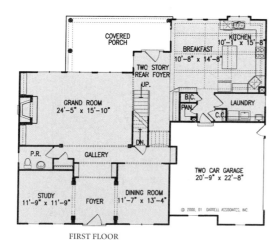

FIRST FLOOR

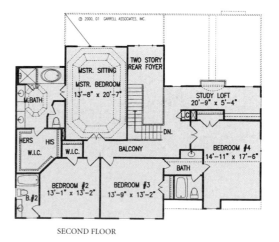

SECOND FLOOR

Textures—rugged and weathered—and natural materials such as cedar shingles, exposed wood trusses, and stone create a cottage design perfectly suited to a coastal forest. From the foyer, take in the well-balanced combination of private, casual, and formal spaces defined by decorative square columns and a sense of function. The study—or guest room—offers seclusion and retreat with a full bath, walk-in closet, fireplace, and built-in shelves. A series of windows invites light and landscape into the great room. A central fireplace is a great place to gather friends and family. An adjoining dining room offers a graceful presentation and features a china or serving alcove. Take a few steps to the right and meet the open C-shaped kitchen. A center island is simply a must-have. A private porch opens to the bedroom and the bath. A second family bedroom enjoys a private bath and walk-in closet.

plan# HPK1800151

Style: Craftsman
First Floor: 2,075 sq. ft.
Second Floor: 1,204 sq. ft.
Total: 3,279 sq. ft.
Bedrooms: 3
Bathrooms: 3½
Width: 63' - 1"
Depth: 58' - 6"
Foundation: Unfinished Walkout Basement

ORDER ONLINE @ EPLANS.COM

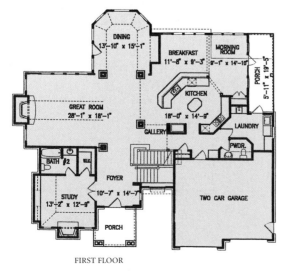

FIRST FLOOR

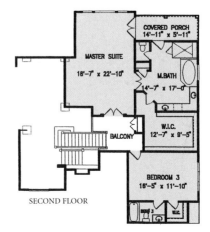

SECOND FLOOR

plan# HPK1800152

Style: Craftsman
First Floor: 2,222 sq. ft.
Second Floor: 1,235 sq. ft.
Total: 3,457 sq. ft.
Bedrooms: 4
Bathrooms: 3½
Width: 70' - 0"
Depth: 100' - 6"
Foundation: Crawlspace

ORDER ONLINE @ EPLANS.COM

Sturdy pillars, stone accents, and gable detailing announce this design's Craftsman influences. Inside, the vaulted great room boasts a fireplace and built-in media center, and opens to the rear property through two sets of doors. Nearby, the breakfast nook—with access to a covered porch—adjoins a spacious island kitchen. The first-floor master suite provides a bay window, two walk-in closets, and a private bath with a compartmented toilet. Upstairs, a second master suite—also with a private bath—joins two additional bedrooms, one of which can double as a study.

FIRST FLOOR

SECOND FLOOR

Interesting window treatments highlight this stone-and-shake facade, but don't overlook the columned porch to the left of the portico. Arches outline the formal dining room and the family room, both of which are convenient to the island kitchen. Household chores are made easier by the placement of a pantry, powder room, laundry room, and office between the kitchen and the entrances to the side porch and garage. If your goal is relaxation, the breakfast room, screened porch, and covered deck are also nearby. The master suite features a beautiful bay. Three secondary bedrooms and a recreation room are on the lower level.

plan# HPK1800153

Style: Craftsman
Main Level: 2,213 sq. ft.
Lower Level: 1,333 sq. ft.
Total: 3,546 sq. ft.
Bonus Space: 430 sq. ft.
Bedrooms: 4
Bathrooms: 3½
Width: 67' - 2"
Depth: 93' - 1"
Foundation: Finished Walkout Basement

ORDER ONLINE @ EPLANS.COM

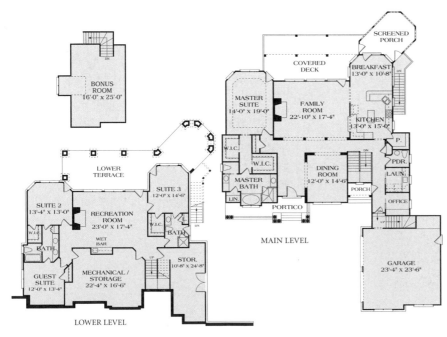

LOWER LEVEL

MAIN LEVEL

REAR EXTERIOR

Open gables with light-catching windows, shed dormers, and stone detailing combine to create an unbeatable Craftsman-influenced facade. The foyer is surrounded by the dining room, study, and living room—find the first of two fireplaces here. The spacious and inviting kitchen is a dream come true—and notice the door leading outside for easy grocery unloading. An office is tucked away near the utility room. The master suite is conveniently located on the first floor, occupying the left side of the home and enjoying dual walk-in closets and a fantastic bath. Three more bedrooms—each with a walk-in closet—reside upstairs.

FIRST FLOOR

SECOND FLOOR

Alluring details such as embellished dormers and stone-and-brick elements lend curb quality to this home's exterior. A formal foyer and dining room are positioned to view the covered front porch. To the rear, the family room—enhanced by a coffered ceiling, built-ins, a bank of windows, and a fireplace—is the perfect spot in which to entertain. For casual times, the keeping room, breakfast space, island kitchen, and screened porch will be the center of activity. The master suite provides a sitting bay, a luxurious bath, and an immense walk-in closet. A vaulted home office sits right across the hall, ready for your most inspiring ideas. Two family bedrooms share a compartmented bath, media desk, and a bonus retreat.

plan # HPK1800155

Style: Bungalow
First Floor: 2,499 sq. ft.
Second Floor: 1,130 sq. ft.
Total: 3,629 sq. ft.
Bedrooms: 5
Bathrooms: 4
Width: 67' - 6"
Depth: 69' - 10"
Foundation: Crawlspace, Unfinished Walkout Basement, Slab

ORDER ONLINE @ EPLANS.COM

FIRST FLOOR

SECOND FLOOR

© 2003 Donald A. Gardner, Inc.

plan# HPK1800156

Style: Craftsman
First Floor: 2,766 sq. ft.
Second Floor: 881 sq. ft.
Total: 3,647 sq. ft.
Bonus Space: 407 sq. ft.
Bedrooms: 3
Bathrooms: 3½
Width: 92' - 5"
Depth: 71' - 10"

ORDER ONLINE @ EPLANS.COM

Using materials that combine the rugged frontier with stately elegance, this home has a grand, majestic facade. Four towering columns frame the dramatic barrel-vault entrance, and clerestories mimic the arched theme. Cedar shake, stone, and siding complement a metal roof over the front porch. The two-story foyer has impressive views of the study, dining room, living room, and balcony. Cathedral ceilings top the family room and master bedroom, and a vaulted ceiling tops the living room. Built-ins, three fireplaces, and a walk-in pantry add special touches. The master suite on the first floor and two family bedrooms upstairs each boast private baths and walk-in closets. A library and flexible bonus space round out the second level.

FIRST FLOOR

SECOND FLOOR

Filled with specialty rooms and abundant amenities, this countryside house is the perfect dream home. Double doors open into an angled foyer, flanked by a music room and a formal great room warmed by a fireplace. The music room leads to the master wing of the home, which includes a spacious bath with a dressing area and double walk-in closet. The great room is the heart of the home—its central position allows access to the island kitchen, formal dining room, and library. Stairs behind the kitchen lead upstairs to a balcony accessing three family bedrooms. The lower level features a billiard room, hobby room, media room, and future possibilities.

plan# HPK1800157

Style: Craftsman
First Floor: 2,782 sq. ft.
Second Floor: 1,027 sq. ft.
Total: 3,809 sq. ft.
Bedrooms: 4
Bathrooms: 4½
Width: 78' - 2"
Depth: 74' - 6"
Foundation: Finished Walkout Basement

ORDER ONLINE @ EPLANS.COM

BASEMENT

FIRST FLOOR

SECOND FLOOR

plan # HPK1800158

Style: Craftsman
First Floor: 2,120 sq. ft.
Second Floor: 1,520 sq. ft.
Third Floor: 183 sq. ft.
Total: 3,823 sq. ft.
Bedrooms: 5
Bathrooms: 4½ + ½
Width: 76' - 0"
Depth: 81' - 0"
Foundation: Finished Walkout
Basement, Slab, Crawlspace

ORDER ONLINE @ EPLANS.COM

The rustic chic of Craftsman details makes this an unusual example of estate architecture. But, extravagant floor planning leaves no doubt that luxury is what this home is about. The first floor has open spaces for living: a reading room and dining room flanking the foyer; a huge family room with built-ins, a fireplace; covered deck access and an island kitchen and nook with built-in table. The first-floor master suite is graced with a beamed ceiling. Its attached bath is well appointed and spacious. On the second floor are four bedrooms and three baths. Third-floor attic space can be used for whatever suits you best. Don't miss the home theater that can be developed in the basement and home-office space over the garage.

OPTIONAL LAYOUT

BASEMENT

FIRST FLOOR

THIRD FLOOR

SECOND FLOOR

Craftsman-style windows and pillars, along with shingles and stone, enhance the exterior of this spacious plan. The open floor plan allows the formal dining room to flow gracefully through a columned area to the two-story great room, which includes a fireplace, built-in media center, and access to the outdoors. The kitchen offers a walk-in pantry, complete with a sink, and adjoins a breakfast nook. A split-bedroom plan on the first floor places the vaulted master suite and its private bath to the right, and an additional bedroom with a walk-in closet to the left. Two second-floor bedrooms have easy access to a den with a wet bar.

plan # HPK1800159

Style: Craftsman
First Floor: 2,950 sq. ft.
Second Floor: 943 sq. ft.
Total: 3,893 sq. ft.
Bedrooms: 4
Bathrooms: 3½
Width: 75' - 0"
Depth: 83' - 0"
Foundation: Crawlspace

ORDER ONLINE @ EPLANS.COM

FIRST FLOOR

SECOND FLOOR

plan# HPK1800160

Style: Craftsman
Main Level: 2,172 sq. ft.
Lower Level: 1,813 sq. ft.
Total: 3,985 sq. ft.
Bedrooms: 4
Bathrooms: 3½
Width: 75' - 0"
Depth: 49' - 0"
Foundation: Finished Walkout Basement

ORDER ONLINE @ EPLANS.COM

With the Craftsman stylings of a mountain lodge, this rustic four-bedroom home is full of surprises. The foyer opens to the right to the great room, warmed by a stone hearth. A corner media center is convenient for entertaining. The dining room, with a furniture alcove, opens to the side terrace, inviting meals alfresco. An angled kitchen provides lots of room to move. The master suite is expansive, with French doors, a private bath, and a spa tub. On the lower level, two bedrooms share a bath; a third enjoys a private suite. The games room includes a fireplace, media center, wet bar, and wine cellar. Don't miss the storage capacity and work area in the garage.

MAIN LEVEL

LOWER LEVEL

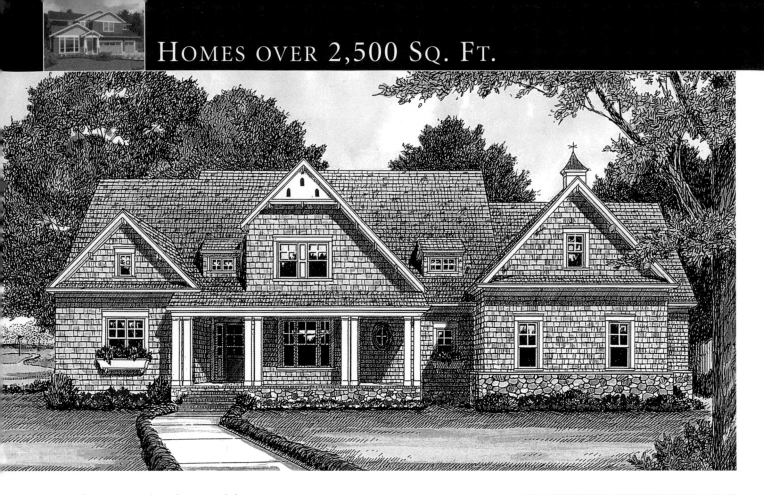

A charming broken gable highlights the facade of this cottage design. The interior layout is perfect for empty-nesters who love to entertain or as a second home near the lake. Decorative columns show off the dining and gathering rooms, dressing up this more formal space. The gourmet kitchen has plenty of room for two or more chefs, and is well-suited for leisurely conversation. The breakfast room enjoys a sunny bank of windows and access to the screened-in porch. The guest room would make a perfect den or home office. Relax in the first-floor master suite outfitted with porch access, twin walk-in closets, and a superb bath. For guests and family, the second level has two suites, an office—or bedroom—bonus room, library, and home theater.

plan# HPK1800161

Style: Craftsman
First Floor: 2,218 sq. ft.
Second Floor: 1,919 sq. ft.
Total: 4,137 sq. ft.
Bedrooms: 4
Bathrooms: 4
Width: 87' - 0"
Depth: 58' - 4"
Foundation: Crawlspace

ORDER ONLINE @ EPLANS.COM

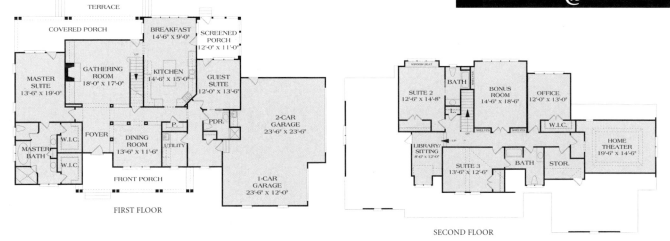

FIRST FLOOR

SECOND FLOOR

plan # HPK1800162

Style: Craftsman
First Floor: 2,572 sq. ft.
Second Floor: 1,578 sq. ft.
Total: 4,150 sq. ft.
Bonus Space: 315 sq. ft.
Bedrooms: 4
Bathrooms: 4½
Width: 78' - 2"
Depth: 68' - 0"
Foundation: Crawlspace

ORDER ONLINE @ EPLANS.COM

Craftsman detailing and a hint of French flair make this home a standout in any neighborhood. An impressive foyer opens to the left to the great room, with a coffered ceiling, warming fireplace, and a charming alcove set in a turret. The kitchen is designed for entertaining, with an island that doubles as a snack bar and plenty of room to move. An adjacent porch invites dining alfresco. The bayed study is peaceful and quiet. A nearby guest room enjoys a private bath. Upstairs, the master suite is awe-inspiring. A romantic fireplace sets the mood and natural light pours in. A sumptuous spa bath leaves homeowners pampered and relaxed. Two bedroom suites share a vaulted bonus room, perfect as a home gym.

SECOND FLOOR

FIRST FLOOR

Take advantage of views on a hilly lot with this raised-foundation design. Craftsman touches outfit this home in rustic character, but the floor plan keeps living spaces entirely modern. Four columns define the foyer and introduce the large gathering room. This space enjoys three sets of French doors, essentially opening the room to the outside. This open floor plan works magic in the kitchen, which serves up an island, pantry, and planning desk. A screened porch sits just off the spacious dining room. The first-floor master suite offers a place to relax. Three family suites, an open study nook, and bonus space creates room for everyone.

plan# HPK1800163

Style: Craftsman
First Floor: 2,533 sq. ft.
Second Floor: 1,820 sq. ft.
Total: 4,353 sq. ft.
Bonus Space: 507 sq. ft.
Bedrooms: 4
Bathrooms: 3½
Width: 85' - 10"
Depth: 81' - 6"
Foundation: Crawlspace

ORDER ONLINE @ EPLANS.COM

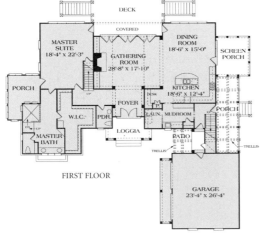

FIRST FLOOR

SECOND FLOOR

plan# HPK1800164

Style: Craftsman
First Floor: 3,072 sq. ft.
Second Floor: 1,406 sq. ft.
Total: 4,478 sq. ft.
Bedrooms: 5
Bathrooms: 4½
Width: 75' - 5"
Depth: 73' - 11"
Foundation: Unfinished Basement

ORDER ONLINE @ EPLANS.COM

A wonderful series of front gables gives the impression that this two-story beauty is bursting with lots of space . . . a perception that is truly accurate. Whether it's the five bedrooms—one an extravagant master suite—or the two-story grand room, a sense of stunning spaciousness reigns. On the first floor, both a library and a home office can be found, along with an expansive gallery hallway and a gracious dining room. For sheer working space and convenience, the island kitchen is extraordinary. It opens easily to a keeping room and large breakfast area that leads to an inviting rear deck.

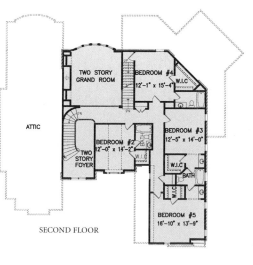

FIRST FLOOR

SECOND FLOOR

The interior of this home boasts high ceilings, a wealth of windows, and interestingly shaped rooms. A covered portico leads into a roomy foyer, which is flanked by an office/study, accessible through French doors. Just beyond the foyer, a huge, vaulted family room highlights columns decorating the entrance and positioned throughout the room. The island kitchen nestles close to the beautiful dining room, which features rear property views through the bay window and a nearby door to the terrace. The main-level master suite enjoys two walk-in closets and a lavish bath, as well as access to a covered terrace. The lower level is home to the remaining bedrooms, including suites 2 and 3, an abundance of storage, a recreation room, and a large mechanical/storage room.

plan # HPK1800165

Style: Craftsman
Main Level: 2,932 sq. ft.
Lower Level: 1,556 sq. ft.
Total: 4,488 sq. ft.
Bedrooms: 3
Bathrooms: 3½ + ½
Width: 114' - 0"
Depth: 82' - 11"
Foundation: Finished Walkout Basement

ORDER ONLINE @ EPLANS.COM

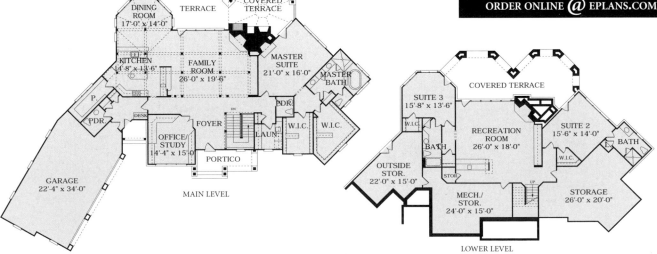

plan# HPK1800166

Style: Craftsman
First Floor: 2,597 sq. ft.
Second Floor: 2,171 sq. ft.
Total: 4,768 sq. ft.
Bedrooms: 4
Bathrooms: 4½
Width: 76' - 6"
Depth: 68' - 6"
Foundation: Crawlspace

ORDER ONLINE @ EPLANS.COM

This splendid Craftsman home will look good in any neighborhood. Inside, the foyer offers a beautiful wooden bench to the right, flanked by built-in curio cabinets. On the left, double French doors lead to a cozy study. The formal dining room is complete with beamed ceilings, a built-in hutch, and cabinets. The large L-shaped kitchen includes a work island/snack bar, plenty of storage, and an adjacent sunny nook. The two-story great room surely lives up to its name, with a massive stone fireplace and a two-story wall of windows. Upstairs, two family bedrooms share a full bath, and the guest suite features its own bath. The lavish master bedroom suite pampers the homeowner with two walk-in closets, a fireplace, and a private deck.

FIRST FLOOR

SECOND FLOOR

PHOTO BY EXPOSURES UNLIMITED, RON & DONNA KOLB. THIS HOME, AS SHOWN IN THE PHOTOGRAPH, MAY DIFFER FROM THE ACTUAL BLUEPRINTS. FOR MORE DETAILED INFORMATION, PLEASE CHECK THE FLOOR PLANS CAREFULLY.

The air of an English Country manor is recreated throughout this home. Repeating interior arches, stone walls, and beamed ceilings are reminiscent of a home created a half-century ago. Highlights include an inviting outdoor summer living room with stone floor, fireplace, wood-beamed ceiling, and the magnificent view it offers. Other exciting features include a large gathering space with kitchen/breakfast room, butler/wine gallery, pub, and hearth room. Views from the entry include the great room, formal dining room, and a library with double doors and built-ins. The first-floor master bedroom pampers with luxury; three upper-level bedrooms—each with private access to a bath and large walk-in closets—make this home the perfect fit for your family.

plan # HPK1800167

Style: Craftsman
First Floor: 3,649 sq. ft.
Second Floor: 1,302 sq. ft.
Total: 4,951 sq. ft.
Bedrooms: 4
Bathrooms: 3½ + ½
Width: 88' - 4"
Depth: 82' - 9"
Foundation: Basement

ORDER ONLINE @ EPLANS.COM

FIRST FLOOR

SECOND FLOOR

plan # HPK1800168

Style: Craftsman
Square Footage: 3,171
Basement: 1,897 sq. ft.
Bedrooms: 5
Bathrooms: 3½
Width: 86' - 2"
Depth: 63' - 8"
Foundation: Finished Walkout Basement

ORDER ONLINE @ EPLANS.COM

A brick, stone, and shake-shingle facade makes this beautiful home a perfect choice for any neighborhood. A large great room, breakfast area, and kitchen create a comfortable and inviting atmosphere. Columns introduce the great room from the foyer, and 12-foot-high ceilings top the great room, breakfast area, kitchen, dining room, and master bedroom. Formal dining is available for special occasions. A covered deck with fireplace and built-in grill offers stylish outdoor living. Angled stairs lead to a lower level where a large party room offers a bar, billiards area, recreation room, and media room. Additional bedrooms are available for the occasional overnight guest.

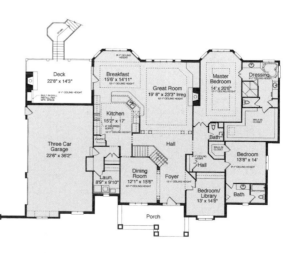

Craftsman style brings to this home a delightful appeal. A wrapping front porch introduces the plan and offers space to enjoy a cool breeze in the evening. The main floor holds great livability with a great room, a club room, a formal dining room, and a tucked-away office. The work center includes an island kitchen with nook and attached sun room, and a craft room is nearby. The second floor holds the master suite and three family bedrooms. The master bedroom has a private deck. An apartment over the three-car garage offers living/dining space, a kitchen, and two bedrooms.

plan # HPK1800169

Style: Craftsman
First Floor: 3,030 sq. ft.
Second Floor: 2,150 sq. ft.
Total: 5,180 sq. ft.
Bedrooms: 4
Bathrooms: 3½
Width: 117' - 6"
Depth: 63' - 6"
Foundation: Crawlspace

ORDER ONLINE @ EPLANS.COM

FIRST FLOOR

SECOND FLOOR

Looks can be deceiving! Although the exterior of this home appears as rustic as a mountain cabin, the interior is nothing but lavish. From a grand foyer, the great room has a warming fireplace and built-in media center. Covered-deck access is perfect year-round, with built-in deck-furniture storage for those colder months. The kitchen is marvelous, with a six-burner cooktop island and a butler's pantry to the dining room, surrounded by glass. The inspiring master suite relishes a luxurious spa bath and tons of natural light. Downstairs, a games room, wine cellar, and theater are special touches. Two generous bedrooms share a full bath and a computer center to the right; to the left, Bedroom 4 enjoys a private spa bath.

LOWER LEVEL

MAIN LEVEL

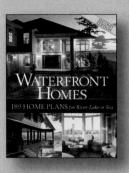

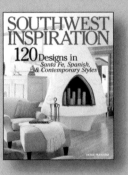
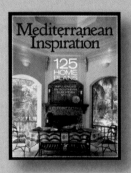

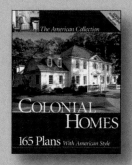

American Collection: Craftsman

Celebrate the fine details and modest proportions of the Craftsman style with this beautiful collection of 165 homes.

$10.95 U.S.
ISBN 1-931131-54-6
192 full-color pages

American Collection: Country

The American Collection: Country is a must-have if you're looking to build a country home or if you want to bring the relaxed country spirit into your current home.

$10.95 U.S.
ISBN 1-931131-35-X
192 full-color pages

American Collection: Colonial

This beautiful collection features distinctly American home styles—find everything from Colonial, Cape Cod, Georgian, Farmhouse or Saltbox.

$10.95 U.S.
ISBN 1-931131-40-6
192 full-color pages

Hanley Wood provides the largest selection of plans from the nation's top designers and architects. Our special home styles collection offers designs to suit any taste.

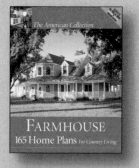

American Collection: Farmhouse

Homes with gabled roofs, wood, stone or glass themes, wrap-around porches and open floorplans make up this wonderful assortment of farmhouse plans.

$10.95 U.S.
ISBN 1-931131-55-4
192 full-color pages

Southern Country, 2nd Ed.

Southern Country Home Plans showcases 300 plans from Historic Colonials to Contemporary Coastals.

$13.95 U.S.
ISBN-10 1-931131-56-2
320 full-color pages

Provençal Inspiration

This title features home plans, landscapes and interior plans that evoke the French Country spirit.

$14.95 U.S.
ISBN 1-881955-89-3
192 full-color pages

Hanley Wood
One Thomas Circle, NW | Suite 600 | Washington, DC 20005
877.477.5450 | www.hanleywoodbooks.com

With more than 50 years of experience in the industry and millions of blueprints sold, Hanley Wood is a trusted source of high-quality, high-value pre-drawn home plans.

Using pre-drawn home plans is a **reliable, cost-effective way** to build your dream home, and our vast selection of plans is second-to-none. The nation's finest designers craft these plans that builders know they can trust. Meanwhile, our friendly, knowledgeable customer service representatives can help you every step of the way.

WHAT YOU'LL GET WITH YOUR ORDER

The contents of each designer's blueprint package is unique, but all contain detailed, high-quality working drawings. You can expect to find the following standard elements in most sets of plans:

I. FRONT PERSPECTIVE

This artist's sketch of the exterior of the house gives you an idea of how the house will look when built and landscaped.

2. FOUNDATION AND BASEMENT PLANS

This sheet shows the foundation layout including concrete walls, footings, pads, posts, beams, bearing walls, and foundation notes. If the home features a basement, the first-floor framing details may also be included on this plan. If your plan features slab construction rather than a basement, the plan shows footings and details for a monolithic slab. This page, or another in the set, may include a sample plot plan for locating your house on a building site. Additional sheets focus on foundation cross-sections and other details.

3. DETAILED FLOOR PLANS

These plans show the layout of each floor of the house. Rooms and interior spaces are carefully dimensioned, doors and windows located, and keys are given for cross-section details provided elsewhere in the plans.

4. HOUSE AND DETAIL CROSS-SECTIONS

Large-scale views show sections or cutaways of the foundation, interior walls, exterior walls, floors, stairways, and roof details. Additional cross-sections may show important changes in floor, ceiling, or roof heights, or the relationship of one level to another. These sections show exactly how the various parts of the house fit together and are extremely valuable during construction. Additional sheets may include enlarged wall, floor, and roof construction details.

5. FLOOR STRUCTURAL SUPPORTS

The floor framing plans provide detail for these crucial elements of your home. Each includes floor joist, ceiling joist, spacing, direction, span, and specifications. Beam and window headers, along with necessary details for framing connections, stairways, or dormers are also included.

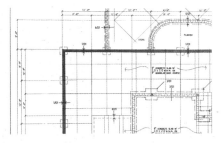

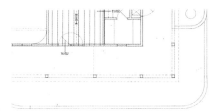

6. ELECTRICAL PLAN

The electrical plan offers suggested locations with notes for all lighting, outlets, switches, and circuits. A layout is provided for each level, as well as basements, garages, or other structures. This plan does not contain diagrams detailing how all wiring should be run, or how circuits should be engineered. These details should be designed by your electrician.

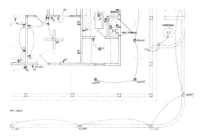

7. EXTERIOR ELEVATIONS

In addition to the front exterior, your blueprint set will include drawings of the rear and sides of your house as well. These drawings give notes on exterior materials and finishes. Particular attention is given to cornice detail, brick and stone accents, or other finish items that make your home unique.

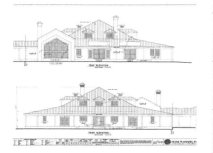

ROOF FRAMING PLANS — PLEASE READ

Some plans contain roof framing plans; however because of the wide variation in local requirements, many plans do not. If you buy a plan without a roof framing plan, you will need an engineer familiar with local building codes to create a plan to build your roof. Even if your plan does contain a roof framing plan, we recommend that a local engineer review the plan to verify that it will meet local codes.

BEFORE YOU CALL

You are making a terrific decision to use a pre-drawn house plan—it is one you can make with confidence, knowing that your blueprints are crafted by national-award-winning certified residential designers and architects, and trusted by builders.

Once you've selected the plan you want—or even if you have questions along the way—our experienced customer service representatives are available 24 hours a day, seven days a week to help you navigate the home-building process. To help them provide you with even better service, please consider the following questions before you call:

■ Have you chosen or purchased your lot?
If so, please review the building setback requirements of your local building authority before you call. You don't need to have a lot before ordering plans, but if you own land already, please have the width and depth dimensions handy when you call.

■ Have you chosen a builder?
Involving your builder in the plan selection and evaluation process may be beneficial. Luckily, builders know they can have confidence with pre-drawn plans because they've been designed for livability, functionality, and typically are builder-proven at successful home sites across the country.

■ Do you need a construction loan?
Construction loans are unique because they involve determining the value of something that is not yet constructed. Several lenders offer convenient contstruction-to-permanent loans. It is important to choose a good lending partner—one who will help guide you through the application and appraisal process. Most will even help you evaluate your contractor to ensure reliability and credit worthiness. Our partnership with IndyMac Bank, a nationwide leader in construction loans, can help you save on your loan, if needed (see the next page for details).

■ How many sets of plans do you need?
Building a home can typically require a number of sets of blueprints—one for yourself, two or three for the builder and subcontractors, two for the local building department, and one or

more for your lender. For this reason, we offer 5- and 8-set plan packages, but your best value is the Reproducible Plan Package. Reproducible plans are accompanied by a license to make modifications and typically up to 12 duplicates of the plan so you have enough copies of the plan for everyone involved in the financing and construction of your home.

■ Do you want to make any changes to the plan?
We understand that it is difficult to find blueprints for a home that will meet all of your needs. That is why Hanley Wood is glad to offer plan Customization Services. We will work with you to design the modifications you'd like to see and to adjust your blueprint plans accordingly—anything from changing the foundation; adding square footage, redesigning baths, kitchens, or bedrooms; or most other modifications. This simple, cost-effective service saves you from hiring an outside architect to make alterations. Modifications may only be made to Reproducible Plan Packages that include the license to modify.

■ Do you have to make any changes to meet local building codes?
While all of our plans are drawn to meet national building codes at the time they were created, many areas required that plans be stamped by a local engineer to certify that they meet local building codes. Building codes are updated frequently and can vary by state, county, city, or municipality. Contact your local building inspection department, office of planning and zoning, or department of permits to determine how your local codes will affect your construction project. The best way to assure that you can make changes to your plan, if necessary, is to purchase a Reproducible Plan Package.

■ Has everyone—from family members to contractors—been involved in selecting the plan?
Building a new home is an exciting process, and using pre-drawn plans is a great way to realize your dreams. Make sure that everyone involved has had an opportunity to review the plan you've selected. While Hanley Wood is the only plans provider with an exchange policy, it's best to be sure all parties agree on your selection before you buy.

CALL TOLL-FREE 1-800-521-6797

Source Key
HPK18

CUSTOMIZE YOUR PLAN – HANLEY WOOD CUSTOMIZATION SERVICES

Creating custom home plans has never been easier and more directly accessible. Using state-of-the-art technology and top-performing architectural expertise, Hanley Wood delivers on a long-standing customer commitment to provide world-class home-plans and customization services. Our valued customers—professional home builders and individual home owners—appreciate the convenience and accessibility of this interactive, consultative service.

With the Hanley Wood Customization Service you can:

■ Save valuable time by avoiding drawn-out and frequently repetitive face-to-face design meetings
■ Communicate design and home-plan changes faster and more efficiently
■ Speed-up project turn-around time
■ Build on a budget without sacrificing quality
■ Transform master home plans to suit your design needs and unique personal style

All of our design options and prices are impressively affordable. A detailed quote is available for a $50 consultation fee. Plan modification is an interactive service. Our skilled team of designers will guide you through the customization process from start to finish making recommendations, offering ideas, and determining the feasibility of your changes. This level of service is offered to ensure the final modified plan meets your expectations. If you use our service the $50 fee will be applied to the cost of the modifications.

You may purchase the customization consultation before or after purchasing a plan. In either case, it is necessary to purchase the Reproducible Plan Package and complete the accompanying license to modify the plan before we can begin customization.

Customization Consultation $50

TOOLS TO WORK WITH YOUR BUILDER

Two Reverse Options For Your Convenience – Mirror and Right-Reading Reverse (as available)

Mirror reverse plans simply flip the design 180 degrees—keep in mind, the text will also be flipped. For a minimal fee you can have one or all of your plans shipped mirror reverse, although we recommend having at least one regular set handy. Right-reading reverse plans show the design flipped 180 degrees but the text reads normally. When you choose this option, we ship each set of purchased blueprints in this format.

Mirror Reverse Fee (indicate the number of sets when ordering) $55
Right Reading Reverse Fee (all sets are reversed) $175

A Shopping List Exclusively for Your Home – Materials List

A customized Materials List helps you plan and estimate the cost of your new home, outlining the quantity, type, and size of materials needed to build your house (with the exception of mechanical system items). Included are framing lumber, windows and doors, kitchen and bath cabinetry, rough and finished hardware, and much more.

Materials List . . . .$85 each
Additional Materials Lists (at original time of purchase only) $20 each

Plan Your Home-Building Process – Specification Outline

Work with your builder on this step-by-step chronicle of 166 stages or items crucial to the building process. It provides a comprehensive review of the construction process and helps you choose materials.
Specification Outline . . . .$10 each

Get Accurate Cost Estimates for Your Home – Quote One® Cost Reports

The Summary Cost Report, the first element in the Quote One® package, breaks down the cost of your home into various categories based on building materials, labor, and installation, and includes three grades of construction: Budget, Standard, and Custom. Make even more informed decisions about your project with the second element of our package, the Material Cost Report. The material and installation cost is shown for each of more than 1,000 line items provided in the standard-grade Materials List, which is included with this tool. Additional space is included for estimates from contractors and subcontractors, such as for mechanical materials, which are not included in our packages.

Quote One® Summary Cost Report $35
Quote One® Detailed Material Cost Report $140*
***Detailed material cost report includes the Materials List**

Learn the Basics of Building – Electrical, Pluming, Mechanical, Construction Detail Sheets

If you want to know more about building techniques—and deal more confidently with your subcontractors—we offer four useful detail sheets. These sheets provide non-plan-specific general information, but are excellent tools that will add to your understanding of Plumbing Details, Electrical Details, Construction Details, and Mechanical Details.

Electrical Detail Sheet $14.95
Plumbing Detail Sheet $14.95
Mechanical Detail Sheet $14.95
Construction Detail Sheet $14.95
SUPER VALUE SETS:
Buy any 2: $26.95; Buy any 3: $34.95; Buy All 4: $39.95

Best Value

MAKE YOUR HOME TECH-READY – HOME AUTOMATION UPGRADE

Building a new home provides a unique opportunity to wire it with a plan for future needs. A Home Automation-Ready (HA-Ready) home contains the wiring substructure of tomorrow's connected home. It means that every room—from the front porch to the backyard, and from the attic to the basement—is wired for security, lighting, telecommunications, climate control, home computer networking, whole-house audio, home theater, shade control, video surveillance, entry access control, and yes, video gaming electronic solutions.

Along with the conveniences HA-Ready homes provide, they also have a higher resale value. The Consumer Electronics Association (CEA), in conjunction with the Custom Electronic Design and Installation Association (CEDIA), have developed a TechHome™ Rating system that quantifies the value of HA-Ready homes. The rating system is gaining widespread recognition in the real estate industry.

Developed by CEDIA-certified installers, our Home Automation Upgrade package includes everything you need to work with an installer during the construction of your home. It provides a short explanation of the various subsystems, a wiring floor plan for each level of your home, a detailed materials list with estimated costs, and a list of CEDIA-certified installers in your local area.

Home Automation Upgrade $250

GET YOUR HOME PLANS PAID FOR!

IndyMac Bank, in partnership with Hanley Wood, will reimburse you up to $600 toward the cost of your home plans simply by financing the construction of your new home with IndyMac Bank Home Construction Lending.

IndyMac's construction and permanent loan is a one-time close loan, meaning that one application—and one set of closing fees—provides all the financing you need.

Apply today at www.indymacbank.com, call toll free at 1-866-237-3478, or ask a Hanley Wood customer service representative for details.

DESIGN YOUR HOME – INTERIOR AND EXTERIOR FINISHING TOUCHES

Be Your Own Interior Designer! – Home Furniture Planner

Effectively plan the space in your home using our Hands-On Home Furniture Planner. It's fun and easy—no more moving heavy pieces of furniture to see how the room will go together. The kit includes reusable peel-and-stick furniture templates that fit on a 12"x18" laminated layout board—enough space to lay out every room in your house.

Home Furniture Planning Kit **$15.95**

Enjoy the Outdoors! – Deck Plans

Many of our homes have a corresponding deck plan, sold separately, which includes a Deck Plan Frontal Sheet, Deck Framing and Floor Plans, Deck Elevations, and a Deck Materials List. A Standard Deck Details Package, also available, provides all the how-to information necessary for building any deck. Get both the Deck Plan and the Standard Deck Details Package for one low price in our Complete Deck Building Package. See the price tier chart below and call for deck plan availability.

Deck Details (only) **$14.95**
Deck Building Package . . . . **Plan price + $14.95**

Create a Professionally Designed Landscape – Landscape Plans

Many of our homes have a front-yard Landscape Plan that is complementary in design to the house plan. These comprehensive Landscape Blueprint Packages include a Frontal Sheet, Plan View, Regionalized Plant & Materials List, a sheet on Planting and Maintaining Your Landscape, Zone Maps, and a Plant Size and Description Guide. Each set of blueprints is a full 18" x 24" with clear, complete instructions in easy-to-read type. Our Landscape Plans are available with a Plant & Materials List adapted by horticultural experts to eight regions of the country. Please specify your region when ordering your plan—see region map below. Call for more information about landscape plan availability and applicable regions.

LANDSCAPE & DECK PRICE SCHEDULE

PRICE TIERS	1-SET STUDY PACKAGE	5-SET BUILDING PACKAGE	8-SET BUILDING PACKAGE	1-SET REPRODUCIBLE*
P1	$25	$55	$95	$145
P2	$45	$75	$115	$165
P3	$75	$105	$145	$195
P4	$105	$135	$175	$225
P5	$175	$205	$305	$405
P6	$215	$245	$345	$445

PRICES SUBJECT TO CHANGE   * REQUIRES A FAX NUMBER

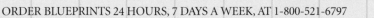

TERMS & CONDITIONS

OUR 90-DAY EXCHANGE POLICY

BUY WITH CONFIDENCE!

Hanley Wood is committed to ensuring your satisfaction with your blueprint order, which is why we offer a 90-day exchange policy. With the exception of Reproducible Plan Package orders, we will exchange your entire first order for an equal or greater number of blueprints from our plan collection within 90 days of the original order. The entire content of your original order must be returned before an exchange will be processed. Please call our customer service department at 1-888-690-1116 for your return authorization number and shipping instructions. If the returned blueprints look used, redlined, or copied, we will not honor your exchange. Fees for exchanging your blueprints are as follows: 20% of the amount of the original order, plus the difference in cost if exchanging for a design in a higher price bracket or less the difference in cost if exchanging for a design in a lower price bracket. (Because they can be copied, Reproducible blueprints are not exchangeable or refundable.) Please call for current postage and handling prices. Shipping and handling charges are not refundable.

ARCHITECTURAL AND ENGINEERING SEALS

Some cities and states now require that a licensed architect or engineer review and "seal" a blueprint, or officially approve it, prior to construction. Prior to application for a building permit or the start of actual construction, we strongly advise that you consult your local building official who can tell you if such a review is required.

LOCAL BUILDING CODES AND ZONING REQUIREMENTS

Each plan was designed to meet or exceed the requirements of a nationally recognized model building code in effect at the time and place the plan was drawn. Typically plans designed after the year 2000 conform to the International Residential Building Code (IRC 2000 or 2003). The IRC is comprised of portions of the three major codes below. Plans drawn before 2000 conform to one of the three recognized building codes in effect at the time: Building Officials and Code Administrators (BOCA) International, Inc.;

the Southern Building Code Congress International, (SBCCI) Inc.; the International Conference of Building Officials (ICBO); or the Council of American Building Officials (CABO).

Because of the great differences in geography and climate throughout the United States and Canada, each state, county, and municipality has its own building codes, zone requirements, ordinances, and building regulations. Your plan may need to be modified to comply with local requirements. In addition, you may need to obtain permits or inspections from local governments before and in the course of construction. We authorize the use of the blueprints on the express condition that you consult a local licensed architect or engineer of your choice prior to beginning construction and strictly comply with all local building codes, zoning requirements, and other applicable laws, regulations, ordinances, and requirements. Notice: Plans for homes to be built in Nevada must be redrawn by a Nevada-registered professional. Consult your local building official for more information on this subject.

TERMS AND CONDITIONS

These designs are protected under the terms of United States Copyright Law and may not be copied or reproduced in any way, by

any means, unless you have purchased a Reproducible Plan Package and signed the accompanying license to modify and copy the plan, which clearly indicates your right to modify, copy, or reproduce. We authorize the use of your chosen design as an aid in the construction of ONE (1) single- or multifamily home only. You may not use this design to build a second dwelling or multiple dwellings without purchasing another blueprint or blueprints or paying additional design fees. Multi-use fees vary by designer—please call one of experienced sales representatives for a quote.

DISCLAIMER

The designers we work with have put substantial care and effort into the creation of their blueprints. However, because we cannot provide on-site consultation, supervision, and control over actual construction, and because of the great variance in local building requirements, building practices, and soil, seismic, weather, and other conditions, WE MAKE NO WARRANTY OF ANY KIND, EXPRESS OR IMPLIED, WITH RESPECT TO THE CONTENT OR USE OF THE BLUEPRINTS, INCLUDING BUT NOT LIMITED TO ANY WARRANTY OF MERCHANTABILITY OR OF FITNESS FOR A PARTICULAR PURPOSE. ITEMS, PRICES, TERMS, AND CONDITIONS ARE SUBJECT TO CHANGE WITHOUT NOTICE.

CALL TOLL-FREE
1-800-521-6797
OR VISIT
EPLANS.COM

IMPORTANT COPYRIGHT NOTICE

From the Council of Publishing Home Designers

Blueprints for residential construction (or working drawings, as they are often called in the industry) are copyrighted intellectual property, protected under the terms of the United States Copyright Law and, therefore, cannot be copied legally for use in building. The following are some guidelines to help you get what you need to build your home, without violating copyright law:

1. HOME PLANS ARE COPYRIGHTED

Just like books, movies, and songs, home plans receive protection under the federal copyright laws. The copyright laws prevent anyone, other than the copyright owner, from reproducing, modifying, or reusing the plans or design without permission of the copyright owner.

2. DO NOT COPY DESIGNS OR FLOOR PLANS FROM ANY PUBLICATION, ELECTRONIC MEDIA, OR EXISTING HOME

It is illegal to copy, change, or redraw home designs found in a plan book, CDROM or on the Internet. The right to modify plans is one of the exclusive rights of copyright. It is also illegal to copy or redraw a constructed home that is protected by copyright, even if you have never seen the plans for the home. If you find a plan or home that you like, you must purchase a set of plans from an authorized source. The plans may not be lent, given away, or sold by the purchaser.

3. DO NOT USE PLANS TO BUILD MORE THAN ONE HOUSE

The original purchaser of house plans is typically licensed to build a single home from the plans. Building more than one home from the plans without permission is an infringement of the home designer's copyright. The purchase of a multiple-set package of plans is for the construction of a single home only. The purchase of additional sets of plans does not grant the right to construct more than one home.

4. HOUSE PLANS IN THE FORM OF BLUEPRINTS OR BLACKLINES CANNOT BE COPIED OR REPRODUCED

Plans, blueprints, or blacklines, unless they are reproducibles, cannot be copied or reproduced without prior written consent of the copyright owner. Copy shops and blueprinters are prohibited from making copies of these plans without the copyright release letter you receive with reproducible plans.

5. HOUSE PLANS IN THE FORM OF BLUEPRINTS OR BLACKLINES CANNOT BE REDRAWN

Plans cannot be modified or redrawn without first obtaining the copyright owner's permission. With your purchase of plans, you are licensed to make non-structural changes by "red-lining" the purchased plans. If you need to make structural changes or need to redraw the plans for any reason, you must purchase a reproducible set of plans (see topic 6) which includes a license to modify the plans. Blueprints do not come with a license to make structural changes or to redraw the plans. You may not reuse or sell the modified design.

6. REPRODUCIBILE HOME PLANS

Reproducible plans (for example sepias, mylars, CAD files, electronic files, and vellums) come with a license to make modifications to the plans. Once modified, the plans can be taken to a local copy shop or blueprinter to make up to 10 or 12 copies of the plans to use in the construction of a single home. Only one home can be constructed from any single purchased set of reproducible plans either in original form or as modified. The license to modify and copy must be completed and returned before the plan will be shipped.

7. MODIFIED DESIGNS CANNOT BE REUSED

Even if you are licensed to make modifications to a copyrighted design, the modified design is not free from the original designer's copyright. The sale or reuse of the modified design is prohibited. Also, be aware that any modification to plans relieves the original designer from liability for design defects and voids all warranties expressed or implied.

8. WHO IS RESPONSIBLE FOR COPYRIGHT INFRINGEMENT?

Any party who participates in a copyright violation may be responsible including the purchaser, designers, architects, engineers, drafters, homeowners, builders, contractors, sub-contractors, copy shops, blueprinters, developers, and real estate agencies. It does not matter whether or not the individual knows that a violation is being committed. Ignorance of the law is not a valid defense.

9. PLEASE RESPECT HOME DESIGN COPYRIGHTS

In the event of any suspected violation of a copyright, or if there is any uncertainty about the plans purchased, the publisher, architect, designer, or the Council of Publishing Home Designers (www.cphd.org) should be contacted before proceeding. Awards are sometimes offered for information about home design copyright infringement.

10. PENALTIES FOR INFRINGEMENT

Penalties for violating a copyright may be severe. The responsible parties are required to pay actual damages caused by the infringement (which may be substantial), plus any profits made by the infringer commissions to include all profits from the sale of any home built from an infringing design. The copyright law also allows for the recovery of statutory damages, which may be as high as $150,000 for each infringement. Finally, the infringer may be required to pay legal fees which often exceed the damages.

BLUEPRINT PRICE SCHEDULE

PRICE TIERS	1-SET STUDY PACKAGE	5-SET BUILDING PACKAGE	8-SET BUILDING PACKAGE	1-SET REPRODUCIBLE*
A1	$465	$515	$570	$695
A2	$505	$560	$615	$755
A3	$570	$625	$685	$860
A4	$615	$680	$745	$925
C1	$660	$735	$800	$990
C2	$710	$785	$845	$1,055
C3	$775	$835	$900	$1,135
C4	$830	$905	$960	$1,215
L1	$920	$1,020	$1,105	$1,375
L2	$1,000	$1,095	$1,185	$1,500
L3	$1,105	$1,210	$1,310	$1,650
L4	$1,220	$1,335	$1,425	$1,830
SQ1				.40/SQ. FT.
SQ3				.55/SQ. FT.
SQ5				.80/SQ. FT.

PRICES SUBJECT TO CHANGE

* REQUIRES A FAX NUMBER

PLAN #	PRICE TIER	PAGE	MATERIALS LIST	QUOTE ONE®	DECK	DECK PRICE	LANDSCAPE	LANDSCAPE PRICE	REGIONS
HPK1800001	C1	6							
HPK1800002	SQ1	8							
HPK1800003	A2	12							
HPK1800004	C1	13							
HPK1800005	A4	14							
HPK1800006	SQ1	15							
HPK1800007	A2	16							
HPK1800008	A2	17	Y						
HPK1800009	A4	18							
HPK1800010	A4	19							
HPK1800011	A2	20							
HPK1800012	A3	21	Y						
HPK1800013	A2	22	Y						
HPK1800014	A4	23							
HPK1800015	A3	24	Y						
HPK1800016	A3	25							
HPK1800017	A3	26	Y						
HPK1800018	C1	27							
HPK1800019	A3	28	Y						
HPK1800020	A3	29							
HPK1800021	A3	30							
HPK1800022	C1	31	Y						
HPK1800023	A3	32							
HPK1800024	A3	33							
HPK1800025	A3	34	Y						
HPK1800026	A4	35	Y						
HPK1800027	A3	36							
HPK1800028	A4	37	Y						
HPK1800029	C1	38							
HPK1800030	A3	39							

PLAN #	PRICE TIER	PAGE	MATERIALS LIST	QUOTE ONE®	DECK	DECK PRICE	LANDSCAPE	LANDSCAPE PRICE	REGIONS
HPK1800031	A3	40							
HPK1800032	C1	41							
HPK1800033	A3	42	Y						
HPK1800034	A3	43							
HPK1800035	C1	44							
HPK1800036	A3	45							
HPK1800037	C1	46							
HPK1800038	A4	47	Y						
HPK1800039	A3	48							
HPK1800040	C1	49							
HPK1800041	A3	50							
HPK1800042	A3	51	Y						
HPK1800043	A4	52	Y						
HPK1800044	A3	53							
HPK1800045	A3	54							
HPK1800046	A3	55							
HPK1800047	A3	56							
HPK1800048	C1	58							
HPK1800049	A3	59	Y						
HPK1800050	C1	60							
HPK1800051	A4	61	Y						
HPK1800052	A4	62	Y	Y					
HPK1800053	C1	63							
HPK1800054	A3	64							
HPK1800055	A3	65							
HPK1800056	C1	66							
HPK1800057	C1	67							
HPK1800058	A3	68							
HPK1800059	A3	69	Y						
HPK1800060	C1	70							

PLAN #	PRICE TIER	PAGE	MATERIALS LIST	QUOTE ONE®	DECK	DECK PRICE	LANDSCAPE	LANDSCAPE PRICE	REGIONS
HPK1800061	A3	71	Y						
HPK1800062	A3	72	Y						
HPK1800063	A3	73							
HPK1800064	A3	74	Y	Y			OLA003	P3	123568
HPK1800065	C2	75							
HPK1800066	A4	76	Y						
HPK1800067	A4	77	Y						
HPK1800068	A4	78							
HPK1800069	A4	79	Y	Y	ODA012	P3	OLA003	P3	123568
HPK1800070	C2	80							
HPK1800071	A4	81	Y				OLA001	P3	123568
HPK1800072	C1	82	Y						
HPK1800073	C2	83							
HPK1800074	C1	84							
HPK1800075	C2	85							
HPK1800076	A4	86							
HPK1800077	C1	87							
HPK1800078	A4	88	Y						
HPK1800079	C2	89							
HPK1800080	C1	90	Y						
HPK1800081	A4	91	Y	Y	ODA017	P2	OLA010	P3	1234568
HPK1800082	C1	92	Y						
HPK1800083	A4	93	Y						
HPK1800084	C1	94	Y						
HPK1800085	A4	95							
HPK1800086	A4	96	Y						
HPK1800087	A4	97							
HPK1800088	A4	98	Y	Y					
HPK1800089	A4	99	Y						
HPK1800090	C1	100							
HPK1800091	A4	101	Y						
HPK1800092	C1	102	Y						
HPK1800093	C2	103							
HPK1800094	A4	104							
HPK1800095	C2	105							
HPK1800096	A4	106							
HPK1800097	C2	107							
HPK1800098	A4	108							
HPK1800099	C2	109							
HPK1800100	A4	110							
HPK1800101	C1	111							
HPK1800102	A4	112							
HPK1800103	A4	113							
HPK1800104	A4	114	Y						
HPK1800105	C2	115							
HPK1800106	A4	116							
HPK1800107	A4	118	Y						
HPK1800108	C1	119							
HPK1800109	C1	120	Y						
HPK1800110	C1	121							
HPK1800111	C1	122	Y						
HPK1800112	C3	123							
HPK1800113	C1	124							
HPK1800114	C1	125							
HPK1800115	C1	126							
HPK1800116	C3	127							
HPK1800117	C1	128	Y						
HPK1800118	C2	129							
HPK1800119	C3	130							
HPK1800120	C2	131	Y						
HPK1800121	C3	132							
HPK1800122	C3	133	Y						
HPK1800123	C1	134							
HPK1800124	C3	135							
HPK1800125	C3	136							
HPK1800126	C3	137							
HPK1800127	C3	138							
HPK1800128	C3	139							
HPK1800129	C1	140							
HPK1800130	C1	141							
HPK1800131	C3	142							
HPK1800132	C2	143							
HPK1800133	C1	144							
HPK1800134	C3	145							
HPK1800135	C2	146	Y						
HPK1800136	C2	147							
HPK1800137	C2	148							
HPK1800138	C1	149	Y						
HPK1800139	C2	150							
HPK1800140	C2	151							
HPK1800141	C4	152							
HPK1800142	C2	153							
HPK1800143	C2	154	Y						
HPK1800144	C2	155							
HPK1800145	C2	156							
HPK1800146	C4	157							
HPK1800147	SQ1	158	Y						
HPK1800148	C2	159							
HPK1800149	C2	160	Y						
HPK1800150	C2	161							
HPK1800151	C1	162							
HPK1800152	C2	163	Y						
HPK1800153	L1	164	Y						
HPK1800154	C3	165							
HPK1800155	L1	166							
HPK1800156	C4	167							
HPK1800157	SQ1	168							
HPK1800158	SQ1	169							
HPK1800159	C3	170							
HPK1800160	SQ1	171	Y						
HPK1800161	L2	172							
HPK1800162	SQ1	173	Y						
HPK1800163	L2	174							
HPK1800164	SQ1	175							
HPK1800165	L2	176							
HPK1800166	C4	177	Y						
HPK1800167	L1	178	Y						
HPK1800168	C2	179	Y						
HPK1800169	L1	180	Y						
HPK1800170	SQ1	181	Y	Y					

With its handsome mix of materials, pleasing geometries, and open spaces, a Craftsman home is all about the details.

SAM GRAY